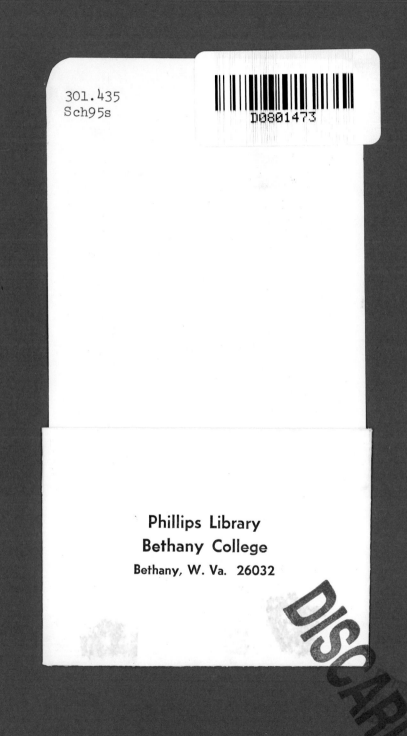

SURVIVAL HANDBOOK FOR
CHILDREN OF AGING PARENTS

Survival Handbook for Children of Aging Parents

DR. ARTHUR N. SCHWARTZ

FOLLETT PUBLISHING COMPANY / Chicago

Jacket/cover designed by Allen Carr.

International Standard Book Number: 0–695–80811–7
Library of Congress Catalog Card Number: 77–81322

This book is dedicated

 *to my middle-aged and elderly clients,*
for their patience with me

 *to Bente, Howard, and Jesse,*
for their impatience with me

 *and to M. D. and Grams,*
who have shown how all this
can work.

Contents

SURVIVAL HANDBOOK FOR
CHILDREN OF AGING PARENTS

Why This Book?

This book is for middle-aged children! That is to say, it was written for those sons and daughters who, having reached mid-life and having pretty much completed the "parenting" of their own children, are now wrestling with the sometimes bittersweet task of understanding and dealing with aging parents.

In the course of my experience as a counselor and therapist in private practice, as well as a teacher and trainer (in a large university) of those who would be counselors of older adults and their families, I have enjoyed the privilege of having middle-aged sons and daughters sit in my office and share with me the worries, fears, frustrations, bewilderment, even conflicts that nag and distress as they struggle to understand and cope with aging kin. Often these sons and daughters have been able to express poignantly the dilemma of being torn between legitimate self-interest and agonizing feelings of guilt. Sometimes they have asked for explanations about the changes they see taking place in the elderly they care about and care for. It seems they have not wanted sympathy so much as useful information to guide them. As often as not they have been hungry for reassurance to quiet the pain.

The difficulty for such seekers has been in knowing where to look for and find useful, nontechnical, broadly applicable information and guidelines. Primarily for these persons is this book intended. Others also may find this book helpful and it may brighten their hopes; some may find it provocative. My best hope is that the book will help enrich relationships between middle-aged sons and daughters and their aging parents. In that respect elderly parents, too, may find some useful things here.

A few decades ago, three or even four generations managed to live together very closely—sometimes even in the same house—each person having his recognized and familiar role. They worked, played, argued, worshiped, struggled, triumphed, and failed together. With rather few exceptions, all that is obviously now changed, for a number of reasons. What is most different is that many more people than ever before are surviving into their sixties, seventies, eighties, and beyond. Middle-agers must therefore come to terms more and more with their aged. In the process there are a great many misconceptions and stereotypes and wrong notions about aging to overcome. Abraham Heschel's ironic comment at a White House Conference on Aging (in 1961) is a sad but true commentary: "Medical science, in conquering disease and enabling us to live longer, had thought it gave us a blessing; we, however, have turned old age into a terrible disease." Of course, it's not *that* at all! Old age need not be a burden to either the elderly or to the middle generation to which they are linked.

The message of this book is that old age can be enormously worthwhile and that the younger generation, by helping to make it so, can draw rich dividends from that fact. You will see, then, that this book is not meant to be a resource book for professionals. Rather, I have tried to envision your sitting down with me and our talking together about such problems as I imagine concern you. There is no catalog of techniques here, no handbook of solutions; certainly the book is not the final answer to all questions on the subject. It is intended as an easy-to-follow guide based on reliable, up-to-date research and on sound common sense and common experience. Most important, I hope it will stimulate you to think about the aged you care about in a different way and from a different perspective than you might have done in the past. If, by so doing, this book helps you care for your elderly in a more insightful, understanding, and appreciative way, and if it helps turn the years of loss into the years of promise, it will serve the purpose for which it was intended.

1

Is It Really Worth It— Growing Old?

THE LONGEVITY PILL, YES OR NO? . . . EXPECTATIONS
ABOUT AGING. . . . AGING STANDARDS—ARE THERE
ANY? . . . MYTHS AND STEREOTYPES ABOUT AGING. . . .
DEPRESSION—A STATE OF MIND, NOT A DISEASE. . . .
SELF-ESTEEM—HOW IMPORTANT? . . . CONSERVING
ENERGY. . . . WHEN TO HELP, AND HOW. . . .
COMPENSATING FOR LOSS.

There is no such thing as a long-life pill. But let's
assume for a moment that scientists had just invented
one. Let's also say that if you took it regularly, you
would be guaranteed to live at least 150 years—or
longer. If there were such a pill available today, would
you take it? I have found that many people, when presented with such a proposition, at first are inclined to
answer, "Yes, indeed, I would take it!" But on second
thought, they are likely to change their answer to,
"Well, it all depends."

"Depends on what?"

"It depends upon how living that long—if it were
possible—would turn out for me."

That's the kind of answer that moves immediately
to the very heart of the issue about living to a ripe,
old age. Generally speaking, most everyone wants to
survive. And, ordinarily, getting older is something
we would welcome with open arms (especially when
you consider the alternative). Curiously enough, the

prospect of aging seems instead to arouse in many people a great deal of apprehension—even dread. Because of a profusion of myths, stereotypes, and fearful images, many people—including older people— have developed baseless and unnecessary fears about growing old. If a life-extending pill were in fact available today, most everyone, it seems, would have very mixed feelings about taking it. Who would want to be able to live 150 years or more if he knew he would likely end up being an incompetent, a misfit, or an invalid—or would be treated like one. Nobody wants that. Yet that nicely illustrates the most basic and pervasive stereotype of old age in our society— namely, that old is incompetent; old is sick; old is being unwanted; old is worn out, tired, useless, and bad. Now that's a pretty dismal picture, but it's not unlike the way "old" is viewed by a great many people today.

On the other hand, if you could be assured that by taking this magic pill, not only could you expect your life to be a lot longer but also continue to be worthwhile—that is, if you could look forward to carrying on most normal activities; if you could continue to have worthwhile things to do of your choosing; if you knew you would continue to have a place and a role in your community; if you continued to have friends who care and someone and some things for you to love; if you continued to have variety in your life and adventure and excitement—wouldn't that make the difference?

Even though it may seem obvious, it is important to begin with some definition of what "makes the difference." When all is said and done, the crucial consideration is not how long you—or your aged—manage to live. The most important thing is whether or not we can live the full measure of our lives with a certain agreeable style, grace, and dignity—and still maintain the capacity for getting satisfaction out of life. A lot depends upon what kinds of expectations you and your elders have about the later years. Many people seem very uncertain as to what they can and should expect of life in old age. The fact is that we just don't have the kinds of standards for old age spelled out for us in orderly fashion the way we have for children. We can find all kinds of books, for instance, that tell us when children can be expected to begin using their fingers effectively or to begin walking, when we can expect them to say the first word or get the first tooth, and so on. Standards for children are even "fine-tuned" to within a matter of weeks. We have a pretty good idea of what to expect (and when to expect it) of young children—or even of adolescents and young adults, for that matter. Given that information, we're likely to expect neither too much nor too little. We simply can't do the same thing for older persons because there are so many differences among persons in their later years.

I said we don't have the same kinds of standards for the elderly as we have for children. But that doesn't mean we don't have *any* expectations. Indeed, we do have expectations about aging. The problem is, most of these expectations tend to be negative ones. Have you noticed how many people seem just a little bit surprised when they run into an elderly person who performs very well or accomplishes a task in an extremely competent fashion, or even appears to function better than mediocre? How many times have you heard it said, "He did very well—for an eighty-year-old"? (That's not much different from the statement

"She did very well—for a woman"!) What we are really saying is that we don't expect persons of that age to do very well. That kind of comment tells us again and again how widespread and ingrained our negative expectations of old age really are. Some people are calling such negative expectations "ageism."

Where do these negative expectations of old age come from? Mostly, I think, they come from myths and stereotypes about old people. Sometimes they come from looking at the wrong things, sometimes from misinterpretation of the facts. Negative expectations also come from the abundant descriptions (including the many horribly belittling stereotyped TV portrayals) we get of sick older people. Clinicians themselves have done their job so well—that is, have exhaustively described and documented the pathologies and losses of old age—that inadvertently they have given old age a bad name and a bad image. Where attention to age has been paid, it has, in the past, been mostly to that special group of sick (especially disabled) elderly that represents only a very tiny proportion of the total older population (perhaps 3 to 5 percent). My point is that we need to pay much more attention to what normal aging is like, or can be, if we want to change our expectations. I sincerely hope this little book will help change some of your expectations about aging and about the old.

It is fair to say, then, that approximately 90 to 95 percent of our aged population is not broken down, is not disabled and senile, but does function capably and is able to carry on—sometimes in the face of tremendous obstacles. We want to look at some of these barriers and obstacles and see how we can reduce or get rid of them. The old among us need all the help they can get! You want to help and that's commendable. You need to make certain you are giving the right kind of help.

Let's be realistic enough to recognize that people in their later years do not carry on exactly as they have in the past. The aging process does make a difference. Being eighty-five years old is not the same as being middle-aged only grown older, any more than little children are small-scale adults. Some very definite changes are closely tied to the process of aging. They do occur and it doesn't do any good to act as if they don't. Growing old does require some accommodations and adjustments. And we want to consider what these are.

Because there has been so much emphasis in discussions of aging on the losses and deficits that go along with old age, many of us have come to take it for granted that old people cannot function very well because of the burden of their years. In sharp contrast to this, we are finding out more and more that a lot of things we used to think were the result of simply getting old are not! They are the effect of events that have little to do with aging as such. They result from intrusions from the outside, or accidents (such as disease); from too much stress; from bad environments; from poor diets; from too little exercise, and the like. In other words, these things are not so much aging problems (although they may be associated with age) as they are human problems that can and sometimes do occur at any time in life, even though they appear more likely to occur in the later years.

For example, consider the particular older person you care about. These comments will necessarily have to be rather general, but perhaps some of these notions will apply. Let's just say that you've always known this older individual to be a fairly enthusiastic, optimistic sort who seemed reasonably content with life. Now, let's say, he (or she, as the case may be) is in his late sixties or seventies, and you begin to notice how frequently he seems to be depressed. It would be natural enough to conclude from your observation that getting old inevitably leads to being depressed. Depression isn't an illness or a disease. In order to understand what's truly happening, you'll surely want to examine what the circumstances are that may lead to that person's feeling depressed. It may be, for instance, that a premature retirement has been forced upon this individual simply because he's celebrated so many birthdays. Now he's left with the feeling of having his life interrupted in an untimely way. It isn't hard to understand how that could contribute a great deal to a feeling of being unwanted and useless. On top of that, if during his earlier years he had never developed hobbies or other interests (work was his whole life), he probably now feels he's facing an empty, boring future, indeed. No special interests, nothing to do, and too much uncommitted time on his hands.

If you want to understand what's happening to him, put yourself in his place. Ask yourself, as he does, if he still counts for very much. A vital question to elderly husbands or wives is what special role they now have within the family circle. Consider, too, what it must be like for them to live now by themselves while the rest of the family is off somewhere else busy with their own lives and careers. Or, if they're living with you, consider what it's like to find it necessary to spend an unusual amount of time in an empty house with not much more to do than watch television all day. If you're working pretty hard and have more than you want to do, and you find yourself dreaming longingly of your next vacation, it may be much too easy to overlook the fact that one curse of the new leisure class, the retired elderly, is boredom! Especially if leisure is involuntary, can boredom and depression be far behind?

In commonsense terms, depression is really not an unusual reaction for any person who has been removed from what has been his or her normal, accustomed role as an income earner, housewife, or involved citizen. Remove any person—young or old—from desired closeness with friends or family or others in the community, and depression can occur. What I want to emphasize is that the problem of depression, looked at in this way, is not so much an aging problem as it is a human problem. Unfortunately, when many older persons go to see a physician, they are often diagnosed as senile or disabled in some way when in fact they are merely depressed. And you may very well be able to do something about that depression, once you discover what gave birth to it in the first place.

Practically any kind of disability provides us with a human problem (common to all ages), as distinct from an aging problem (unique to old age). I think the best illustration of this is the loss of one's self-esteem. There is a universal need to maintain one's self-esteem—to look at oneself and one's life, at least overall, in a positive, accepting way. No matter what issue we choose to talk about—whether it's health, education, housing, transportation, diet, or marriage—the bottom line (as accountants like to say) is the matter of self-esteem. And maintaining our self-esteem very clearly is a task in which we all have a very deep investment, no matter what our chronological age. It's not difficult to see how a personal crisis of esteem can arise because of circumstances associated with growing old in our society.

I think we cannot experience anything but heartache when we observe how self-esteem in any individual—and especially the old—is sometimes slowly eroded and destroyed by life's circumstances.

This business of self-esteem is so important that I want to underline it by quoting from a remarkable lady, Florida Scott-Maxwell, born in 1883. At the age of eighty-four she wrote, in her insightful little book, *The Measure of My Days* (Knopf, 1968), the following poignant words:

> The admonition "Have a proper respect for yourself" or "Your self-respect should have told you what to do" were both based on the assumption that you are of fine quality. . . . Almost everyone makes the assumption; it can be a calamity when it is lacking. . . . Self-protection, self-preservation, these are words that ought to satisfy, but they do not seem to convey that passionate conviction that one can, and should, stand by what one is, but may not seem to be. . . . Who has the right to say what another is? It is here that I feel the conviction lies that we, the simplest and vaguest of us, know that we are other and better than we appear. (pp. 121–22)

Among the many problems to be contended with, of course, are the myths about old age, which have grown like weeds in an untended garden. A very typical instance is the adage "You can't teach an old dog new tricks." We have learned by this time that this myth ought to be finally and completely laid to rest. The fact is that if older people are intrigued by a given task, if they are especially interested in or turned on by something, if they are given full opportunity to work at their most comfortable pace, and if other things are equal, they indeed can learn very well. In certain instances they can learn better than a younger individual. No one's personality or mental ability is set in concrete. People at any age can and do change, and they can continue to learn in old age. The key lies in motivation.

You can't talk about motivation without talking about incentive. Obviously, there is little incentive for learning if the task appears to be overwhelming or if it doesn't jibe with one's interests or if it's a task that appears to be simply busywork. In other words, no activity is going to be very attractive to an older person if it's seen as done just to kill time. What often happens is that older people are given dull "artsy-craftsy" tasks such as coloring egg cartons and tying them together with yarn to make wastebaskets—tasks in which they have no interest and that provide no real incentive. The net result is an oldster who doesn't seem to learn well because he gets bored and gives it up. The fact that older people don't object strenuously to such tasks may only be because they just don't have the energy to fight. It may be much easier at the moment to go through the motions—to go along.

You'll recall some very clear examples of meaningless work that occurred in recent years when young people dropped out of college, even high school. Many who did so were smart enough. They dropped out, they said, because they were disenchanted with or didn't have much interest in the subjects they were offered. Sometimes (too late!) we discovered that the reason many of these young people weren't tuned in to higher education was not because they were incapable of learning but because they weren't properly motivated. What was true of these youngsters and young adults is no less true of an older generation. It gets to be even worse for the elderly because, while we (as a society and as parents) often try very hard to uncover other options for the young, our behavior toward the old often implies that they are simply obsolete. And we let it go at that.

I hope you find that just as appalling and unacceptable as I do. Only if you do are you likely to begin to do something about it—especially for that older person you care about. This leads us to another point I think will help you get a better perspective on aging. It's worth keeping in mind that most of those who plan the programs for older people, most of those who do the research on aging, even many who do much of the talking about old age, turn out to be middle-aged and young people. They're really outsiders and can be said to be looking in on old age because they haven't yet had that experience.

Middle-aged people have personal knowledge of what it's like to be a youngster, a teenager, or a young adult because they've lived through those periods of life. The real experts on old age are those who have completed the package or who are in the process of living the later decades of life. Trouble is, those who have completed the package are not available to us because they've passed on. The others who *are* available are often not consulted or listened to. I don't want you to think that this wipes out or invalidates everything middle-aged and young persons do or say with regard to aging. Nor does this in any sense invalidate careful research on aging. I am only insisting that you carefully consider how important it is that we get as much information as we can about older people *from them* regarding their own experiences and perceptions, which is what conscientious researchers try very hard to do in a systematic way.

We have to take into account at the same time the real possibility that we may get misinformation from elderly people simply because they, too, are the products of their time and their upbringing. There is no question that many elderly people themselves strongly subscribe to stereotypes and mythologies about aging. We must be careful, therefore, not to accept every bit of information uncritically (including the information offered in this book). What we want to get, of course, is the kind of information that is as close as possible to the essential truths about aging in our world and our society and which doesn't merely reflect some variation on old wives' tales. That's where good research comes in and why it can be enormously helpful to us because it does compare, test, and help organize information. Good research can give us some important perspectives on relatively large numbers of older persons who are telling us what old age is all about from the vantage point of the later years. From them we discover that there are so many differences among people as they grow older—a variety in tastes, interests, styles, likes, capabilities, dislikes, energies, and all the rest.

Once we understand that there are enormous variations, we begin to realize that there does not appear to be any one truth or any one reality about aging that applies in the same way to all. One certainty is that there are many ways aging can be described and many ways it is experienced, depending on individual differences. In spite of this, we can identify some common threads of experience. In the end, you will have to make your own specific applications to the older persons you care about.

A middle-aged man sat in my office one day. He was very earnest and convincingly sincere about his concern as he described his "problem" in the following way:

> I remember my parents, who are now in their seventies, when they were optimistic, vibrant, involved people. And that's just twenty years ago. Now I see them very much slowed down, sometimes embarrassingly forgetful, depending on me a little more . . . somehow they don't seem . . . well . . . as effective as they once were. It really breaks my heart to see this happen to them as they go downhill.

We need to examine such events and try to understand them better. For one thing, I believe we do not have to describe such occurrences as without exception downhill. Such behaviors are changes and show us that things are different from what they were. But are they necessarily downhill? By the same token, are all technological changes in our society truly evidence of progress? Many doubt this.

First of all, let us recognize what an irresistible temptation it is to compare an older person we know and care about (whether parent, relative, or friend) as we know him now with how we remember him "then." More than likely, in our minds that older person is going to suffer by such comparisons. Why? Simply because some things (often many things) are quite different now. Older people, for instance, are not as energetic as they once were. But often they have developed, on the basis of experience, better strategies and shortcuts than they had formerly for coping with problems efficiently and with less expenditure of energy. We may see only the slackening of powers, but the truth is there is much more going on than that. There doesn't seem to me to be anything wrong with "thinking young"—so long as it doesn't turn into a collective delusion, namely, that being older is the same as being less effective.

The bald truth about aging is that as we move across the years, a great many changes are taking place. And many, if indeed not most, of these changes can be accurately described as losses. Invariably these losses begin to occur, not at seventy-six years, or sixty-three, or even fifty-five, but much earlier in life than we sometimes suspect or ever care to admit even to ourselves. What we need to come to terms with is that such losses do invite a trade-off—some losses, some gains!

Some of these changes—certainly those of appearance—are quite obvious: thinning and graying of the hair, wrinkles around the face and neck, sagging muscles (due to loss of muscle tone, which comes from too little exercise), liver spots on the face and the back of the hands, and the like. But are these necessarily marks of disfigurement? Beauty is still in the eye of the beholder. Wrinkles can be character lines and gray hair can provide a look of distinction.

Many losses are not very evident at first because they take place, ordinarily, so very, very gradually. Hearing tends to become gradually less acute than it was. While the individual does not necessarily become deaf, one may begin to notice that he will miss a word or a phrase in a conversation here and there, especially when some background noise is present. One day, in a terrible moment of awareness, a person realizes how difficult it is to follow the conversation. The real embarrassment for one with some hearing loss comes in having to face the strange looks of those who are staring back in a puzzled way.

Another gradual change that tends to take place is that eyesight isn't as sharp as it was. One aspect of this is that it takes longer for the eyes to adapt when going from a bright light into a dimly lit or dark place (like a theater). Not only that, it may be harder and more discouraging to try to read signs at a distance or to read books and newspapers close up. Such losses call for glasses, or thicker glasses, and perhaps bifocals.

But that isn't all your older person may have to contend with. In fact, all the senses are likely to be affected in the course of time, including touch, smell, and taste. For example, we are told that by the time we get to be about eighty-five years of age, we are likely to have about 4 percent of the taste buds left that we had at age five. That means that even discounting the effects of other factors such as excessive use of tobacco or alcohol, old familiar foods and drink—even water—are not likely to taste quite the same. The older tongue, with its fewer taste buds, becomes less sensitive to sweet and more sensitive to bitter and sour. That means that if one day you hear some old-timer remark that nothing tastes any more like Mom's apple pie used to, the truth is that for him Mom's apple pie can never again taste quite as he remembers it.

So it goes with the normal losses experienced in the process of aging. I am not going to try to detail all these losses here. I think it more important to get you to consider in what ways these losses can not only affect the older person's sense of himself, but also how they can affect his or her relationship with you and with others.

I experienced one situation where two middle-aged daughters, eager to do the right thing by their elderly mother and encouraged by friends to keep Mother involved and busy, hit upon the notion of urging their mother to begin baking again in her kitchen. This was one thing she used to do expertly. But she hadn't done much of that since the children were grown and she had become a widow.

So she began once again to bake some of her old specialties—cookies and cakes and an occasional pie, which she then offered with some pride to her daughters when they came to visit her in her small apartment. Her daughters adamantly declined to eat any of Mother's baked goods. They insisted, firmly but politely, that the rich goodies were really bad for their strict diets. But Mother had tasted her own handiwork and felt it did not come up to her former standards. She interpreted her daughters' refusal as a sign that they really thought, as she did, that the baked goods were rather tasteless and that she had finally lost her touch. All of this, not too surprisingly, caused Mother to stop cooking and fall into a very blue mood. Nor was this trying situation helped by the fact that the daughters, in turn, took the view that Mother had turned into a cranky old lady and was really acting paranoid. So there we have it—a family relationship needlessly turned sour because of a few thousand lost taste buds and a lot of misunderstanding.

Growing old involves many kinds of physical losses; some are plain to see and others not so evident because they are hidden at the level of tissues and cells. The whole physical system gets involved. The bones, for example, tend to become more brittle and even to shrink a little (so that one may end up being a tiny bit shorter at ninety than one was at thirty-five). Many older people don't breathe as deeply as they did once (partly because posture is poor)—a situation that begins to affect the whole circulatory system. This can make it even more difficult for older people to engage in regular exercise. They may even be a little uncomfortable in doing so, especially when the connective tissue in the joints tends to become a little stiffer, less elastic.

But very careful research is opening the door to new opportunities for well-being. We are learning all over again that appropriate exercise for the old is not only pleasurable but necessary. The old notion that elderly persons should be encouraged—even exhorted—to rest, relax, take it easy, and the like is usually bad advice. Even those who have had heart attacks or have other physical constraints can learn to counter pain and discomfort with the right kind and amount of exercise.

That little old lady who wants her shawl wrapped around her shoulders when all the younger people in the room are insisting on how comfortable it is may not be simply a complaining old lady when she talks about the chill in the air. She may in fact be more vulnerable to temperature change. She is experiencing, as many older people do, the loss of some of the fatty tissue just below the skin, which reduces body insulation (as well as encourages wrinkles).

Or you may wonder why an elderly person seems to sleep so lightly and wake so easily. You may find it rather annoying to discover your oldster wandering around the house at 3:00 or 4:00 A.M. You know, of course, that some people get along with much less sleep than others. Beyond that, more than a few older people have the opportunity as well as the inclination to take catnaps during the day, and they may go to bed rather early in the evening—from years of habit or out of sheer boredom. Equally important to understand in this connection is the fact that a rise of body temperature of as little as one degree is sufficient to awaken some people from sleep. The wandering around at night, therefore, may simply be that individual's spontaneous and unwitting attempt literally to cool the body off. The problem in that case may be too many blankets on the bed or not enough ventilation and too warm a room.

One family I knew invited Grandpa to come stay with them. Grandpa usually went to bed shortly after sundown. To the great annoyance of the family, he would awaken around 3:00 or 4:00 A.M. and then disturb other members of the family by wandering around the house, bumping into chairs, turning on lights, and the like. The problem was at least temporarily solved when the grandson came home from college and almost every evening would engage Grandpa in a game of chess or induce him to watch the late show on TV. Getting to bed at 11:00 P.M. or later meant that Grandpa, now very tired, would sleep like a log until time for breakfast.

All of this is meant to touch on, in a very brief fashion, some of the many different physical changes that do take place as one grows older and to indicate how changes can and do to some degree influence the individual's behavior. What is of greater significance, however, is the fact that such physical changes and multiple losses are a growing and constant reminder to the aging person that his physical machinery, so to speak, no longer functions smoothly, effortlessly, and effectively as it did formerly. All of this is calculated to produce a growing sense of *vulnerability* in the aging person.

Let me suggest a simple little exercise you can try that will help you better appreciate what the experience is like for many older persons. Take any piece of scratch paper and with your pen, or pencil, in the hand opposite that which you ordinarily use (if right-handed, use your left hand; if left-handed, use your right), write (don't print) your name, address, and a few words that describe how it makes you feel to do a familiar task in an unfamiliar way. Remember, use the opposite hand! If you can write equally well with either hand, this won't work, of course. You can immediately see how difficulty with a physical task can have emotional impact—how it can make one *feel* self-conscious, awkward, silly, frustrated, childish, stupid, and even angry.

Most of the losses we are talking about ordinarily occur so very gradually that most people do not immediately notice some of the changes in their vision, hearing, taste, or other senses. Most of the time there is no single, dramatic incident. What is more likely to happen is that one might be looking in a mirror one day and suddenly find himself saying, "I'm getting a lot of gray hairs"; or be driving on the freeway one day and think, "I can't see as well as I used to"; or while attending a movie one night, say to himself,

"Good heavens, I'm having trouble hearing." The losses occur in a very gradual, even subtle, way.

The second important point about these losses is that they don't occur to the same degree and at the same rate in every person. There are tremendous variations among individuals, and it's a serious mistake to assume anything else. It is not a rarity to find an eighty-year-old with near perfect eyesight or a seventy-three-year-old with very good hearing. This variability among individuals and within each individual is one of the most striking facts about people in the later years of life.

There is one thing you can most reliably anticipate about growing old (and can observe as a universal phenomenon in older people around you). That is the tendency to slow down. That's another way of stating that you just don't have the same amount of energy available to you in the later years as you did when you were younger. No doubt you have noticed repeatedly how your older person has in later years become much more careful and much more deliberate in posture, in walking, in getting up and sitting down, in talking—in fact, in all his responses. While you may be inclined to label this slowing down as a loss or deficit, another way of looking at it is to see it as one way the individual has for adapting to the loss of energy reserves. Thus the older person does—indeed *must*—become much more selective of activities due to the now limited reserves of energy available.

The contrast is dramatic when you compare this behavior to that of young children. The healthy eight-year-old is utterly spendthrift with his energies. He doesn't walk when he can run. He doesn't sit in a chair; he throws himself in. The older person rarely, if ever, acts that way. Rather, he carefully—almost like a miser—doles out his use of energy as he does of time. If you want to make sense out of your oldster's behavior, you have to understand this rationing of energy for what it is and not misread it.

In addition to dwindling reserves of energy, there is another factor that needs consideration. Perhaps you find yourself wondering why your older relatives no longer invest the same time and energy in activities or even in certain relationships that they once did. You might consider the possibility that those activities or relationships may no longer have the same degree of interest or meaning as in the past. They may not have as high a priority in the life of that older person as once upon a time. And so the older person does not invest as much physical and emotional energy. If you sometimes wonder why many older people seem too ready to submit passively to certain kinds of indignities, you can remind yourself that the days of dwindling reservoirs of energy are upon them. What you are noticing, then, in the slowing down and in the more deliberate movements is a process of *adaptation* to a particular life circumstance.

I suppose a very natural question in this connection is, Isn't this a time when older people begin to need a great deal of assistance or help? Well, middle-aged offspring and others who care can most certainly be helpful. Surely there's no argument about whether or not you should try to be as helpful as you can. But I believe a word of caution is appropriate here. The major difficulty is how to determine what is truly helpful and when to be helpful. It is possible to go beyond being helpful and offering assistance and end up taking over and doing for the older person what he can do for himself.

The real tragedy of trying to *manage* an older person's life is that the outcome almost always is that the older person is infantalized. The older person gets treated as a baby (which he is not!) and damage is done to his self-esteem (which is most destructive of all!). Grandma, for example, might accomplish a task much more slowly than you would prefer. She might not always be able to do it as effectively as you could because of her physical limitations. She may not do it in the order you would prefer or to suit your taste. Nevertheless, Grandma needs—desperately needs—to be encouraged to pursue and complete her tasks with at least some feeling of competence and effectiveness. Only when it becomes very clear that a given task will continue to be a source of embarrassment to her and will lead to loss of dignity and self-respect on her part will your help be timely. In that case, you can be assured it's help and not infantalizing.

Reversal of roles, no matter how rationalized, practically always turns out to be uncalled for and inappropriate. It practically always ends up demeaning the elderly parent. Our practical experience as well as our common sense tells us that this is a sound principle, even though we may be able to point to the rare exception that merely proves the rule. I realize, too, that this may well sound like too simplistic a principle for problems that may result from complex and difficult circumstances.

Self-esteem (we always need to come back to it) is so basic and important an ingredient in the total life satisfaction of the elderly that we have to start at the point at which it begins to develop—during those first months following birth. From then on, self-esteem is built upon literally hundreds and thousands of big and little events, like the warm cuddling of the infant during and after feeding; the cooing, patting, fondling, and hugging; the squeezes and bouncing on the knees; the pats on the head and words of approval; the good report cards in school; the secrets shared between trusted childhood friends; being chosen to play on a team; being asked to go to a party; hand-holding and smiling between girl friends or boy-friends; promotions in school, the award of a diploma, and later, the reward of a certificate; being hired for a job and getting promotions; still later being asked to take on some responsible job in the community; being asked to serve on a committee; and getting awards to hang on a wall or a trophy to place on a shelf.

These are but a tiny sample of the many events that demonstrate our increasing sense of mastery and control over our environment. These kinds of things bear an important message to the individual—"You are effective, you count, you make a difference, you have impact, you are important!" Thousands of such commonplace experiences—some of them more dramatic, some of them less so—all link together to tell the average person, "You and your life are worthwhile." Such experiences are all bricks in the foundation upon which self-esteem stands.

Quite clearly those losses that surface during the middle years and begin to add up in the later years of life (some of which we have already discussed) convey messages quite different from those that build self-esteem. We've gone over some of the physical losses. We must add to these the experience of social losses.

For example, one price you pay for surviving to one hundred is that all those you have grown up with are gone—partly because of moving from one place to another, sometimes because of divorce or death. Thus that familiar and supporting cluster of family and friends gets broken up and often seriously so. That's why we find the commonest complaint of many older people is that of loneliness.

But our list isn't complete yet. In addition to physical and social losses, there are also economic and vocational losses. Forced retirement (or mandatory unemployment) as we know it not only cuts people off from a familiar group of co-workers and friends. It not only says "You're not needed or useful to us any more," but frequently forces the older individual into poverty or near-poverty. Everyone knows how painfully discouraging it is trying to compete in the open job market beyond the age of sixty—or even fifty or forty-five for that matter. And pensions are not commonplace. Well-paying pensions are even more rare—unless one happens to have been a politician or to have worked for the government.

The many losses of these later years can have severe emotional and psychological consequences, especially if there's nothing to make up for or compensate for such losses. And you need to look for that in the life of your oldster if you want to understand what's going on. Because they run counter to those rewarding and supporting experiences that build self-esteem, these losses tend to reinforce the feeling that the oldsters don't have as much impact and are not as effective, not as useful, not as competent, not as much needed or wanted, and perhaps are not even as worthwhile as they once felt they were. And this kind of feeling about one's self, if intense enough and persistent enough, can damage self-esteem beyond repair. This kind of loss without question is far more destructive to the human spirit than any other loss you can imagine.

Self-esteem and the human spirit is the central theme of this book. There is a lot of evidence to support my argument that you can contribute enormously to helping your older person keep his spirit. The trick of the game is to compensate—to the maximum extent imaginatively possible—for multiple losses that do occur. The central issue for you, then, is not how many losses you count up, not the kinds of pathologies or the extent of the deficits. You couldn't do better than by beginning to identify the visible as well as hidden capabilities of your oldster for getting along, at the very least, well enough to maintain his sense of dignity and self-worth.

Compensating for loss is not an impossible dream. As a matter of fact, we are surrounded by all sorts of examples of precisely this notion when it comes to things we attach to the body. For example, I happen to wear glasses and have done so continuously for approximately thirty-five years (which is about as chronic as a disability can get). There is no question that my eyes are bad. Nor would I challenge for a moment the Department of Motor Vehicles's restriction that I not drive a car without my glasses. But one can easily see that once I put on that prosthetic device known as my glasses, I can see the world around me pretty much as all those blessed with natural 20/20 vision. And if I lost a leg, what would you do or recommend for me? Why, of course, an artificial, or prosthetic, limb. And we all know that when properly fitted and trained in its use, a person can walk, run, work, play, make love, swim, climb—do all sorts of normal things with the help of such a compensating device.

But that's only the beginning. There are so many things that we attach to the body (temporarily or permanently) that serve as compensations for some kind of loss. By making up for a specific loss, the individual can begin to perform or do things capably once again. Isn't that, in fact, what a heart pacer does? And when you consider all the possibilities, isn't that what padded bras and hairpieces and false teeth and girdles do? Aren't they truly compensating devices?

If, by chance, you have been taken aback by my suggestion—indeed, my insistence—that we must try to give back or make up for losses experienced by older persons, don't be. What I have been asking you to consider is that we already have had for some time models at hand for doing this very thing. We have available and do use such things as glasses, hearing aids, prosthetic limbs, heart pacers, cardiac shunts, canes, wheelchairs, walkers, and so on. It's surely not too big a leap to think seriously and imaginatively about how we can extend this idea of compensation into other areas of life for our aged kin. Don't believe for a moment that your concerns about an elderly parent or friend will leave you helpless or without recourse. They needn't at all.

Another way of looking at the same thing is that you are going to be able to offer much more effective help to your elderly parent if you do not allow barriers and obstacles to get in their way. We simply cannot, as we have somewhat insensitively and rather mindlessly done up to now, allow older persons to be penalized simply because they experience losses and have some limitations. We would not think of making it *more* difficult than it is for little children to get along by designing a classroom or a nursery school that doesn't fit them and their particular needs at that period of their lives.

Clearly, what is at stake here is not only the self-esteem but also the physical health and emotional well-being of your older person. If Uncle Charlie is forced to live in a place (whether home or institution) where obstacles make it extremely difficult for him to function except as an invalid, where there are very few landmarks and cues for getting around the place, where things are stored in places hard to get to, where furniture is a disaster because the sofas are much too soft and seats are too low or without arms (have you ever watched an elderly person with arthritis struggle to get up out of a chair that is too deep and has no arms?), where doorknobs are too hard to be turned by an arthritic hand, where electrical outlets can be reached only by getting on your knees, or where the light is too dim for reading and reading materials have such small print that it's discouraging even to try—I say, where Uncle Charlie has to struggle against such tremendous odds, he is predictably going to end up the loser in the struggle. But our elderly Uncle Charlies and Aunt Minnies don't have to end up losers at all!

Pretty clearly, inventing a longevity pill is not going to be the final or total answer. Nor, I suppose, would we expect a youth pill to be the answer either, unless one is prepared to remain seventeen years old indefinitely. The more relevant and practical theme in all of this is, What makes life worthwhile? After all, what makes life worthwhile for someone in the later years is no different from what makes life worthwhile at any age. What makes it worthwhile for you to get up in the morning? Doesn't worthwhileness have to do with feeling useful and effective, having something to do of real significance to you (a job? a hobby?), activities and people that interest you, feeling needed, experiencing adventure, variety—aren't all these the spice of life? No one loses these needs just because of the added years or because of disabilities or because memory gets slippery. Not unless they've literally given up out of sheer frustration. Certainly these needs are not limited to people with high IQs, high incomes, college educations, or important political connections.

More and more people are surviving past childhood as well as getting by some of the killers in middle age. Some studies show that the greatest increase in proportion of the population over the past couple of decades is in the seventy-five-years-plus range. In fact, if those who study population trends are correct (that is, if all their calculations and assumptions hold steady), we can expect that by the turn of the century —in the year 2000—very close to 50 percent of our population will be fifty years of age or older.

What will the quality of our lives be like then? That, of course, is the crucial question. But today's elderly— your elderly—can't wait for the turn of the century. Quality of life is crucial for them right now!

2

Is Senility a Deceiving Mask— or the True Face of Old Age?

If your experience isn't much different from that of many others who care for elderly relatives or friends, in all likelihood you, too, have noticed some changes in their life-styles. Probably you hadn't expected this. Possibly there have even been some drastic changes in behavior, and if these things seem to happen for no reason at all, it must worry and concern you.

Is this the beginning of what is called senility? Are these the first signs of mental incompetence in old age? The problem may not lie in what you observe! That is, you may be seeing things accurately enough, but there is a problem in making a fair and reasonably accurate determination of what the behavior means, what it signifies.

We need to pay attention to what we mean by senility and then discuss the issue of mental incapacity in old age. There is great difficulty in defining the word *senility* simply because it has no precise meaning. Furthermore, it is not a medical diagnosis, in spite of the fact that many physicians (and others) often use the word as if it were. It is a kind of wastebasket word—much like the term *mental illness* or *dementia*—and loosely refers to certain descriptions of certain behavior. Maybe you've heard the old saw that goes like this: "There are three major signs of senility. The first is loss of memory—and I can't seem to recall the other two." Well, it's no joke, because that refers to a very common human experience.

The more sobering fact is that the term *senility* (unlike the word *senescence*, which means "the process of growing old") seems to have taken on much of the flavor of the word *cancer;* it arouses in many people an enormous amount of apprehension and anxiety. At worst, it can strike terror in the heart, about which many a son or daughter can testify. To most people the word *senility,* like the word *mental illness,* or *dementia,* means "going crazy." At best, it means being a little addled in old age. Sad to say, even some professionals continue to perpetuate the anxiety by continuing to use the word *dementia* in connection with the word *senility.*

The idea of senility is based mainly on facts of behavior like memory loss, disorientation (not knowing where one is, inability to recognize or identify a familiar person, or not knowing the date or the time), confusion, and the like. But when it comes to understanding and dealing with an older person who exhibits such behavior, it is important to determine what causes that kind of behavior before applying what is at best a very bad label.

Here is a true story—to illustrate the point. A few years back a friend of mine told me how shortly after taking a position as psychiatrist in a large state hospital, he found himself almost overwhelmed by complaints from members of the staff regarding an elderly inmate (a man in his eighties) who, they said, was a particularly disturbing management problem. Staff complaints consisted largely of his appearing frequently confused, disoriented, uncooperative, and untidy. But what was most distressing of all to the staff (and understandably so) was the fact that in spite of many admonitions from them, he persisted from time to time in urinating on the walls of the hospital dayroom, where he spent much time. Obviously, this old man was "senile"—or fast becoming that—and the staff wanted help, urgently!

The psychiatrist arranged to have a long talk with this gentleman and this is what he uncovered. The old man had lost his family in recent years and subsequently found himself moved in and out of several long-term care facilities, the last being a state hospital. This place was even more strange to him than the others had been, and he had a lot of trouble finding his way around. This situation was not helped by the fact that he had very poor vision. The routines of the institution were unfamiliar and confused him.

Each morning a kindhearted fellow inmate helped him find his way through the maze of corridors to their very large dayroom (a standard feature in old state hospitals), where he spent a good part of the day.

Three or four sixty-watt bulbs hung at intervals from the ceiling in this enormous room, which was painted in its entirety a dismal brindled color except for several old-fashioned steam radiators that hung on the walls. These were painted silver and gleamed a little in the dim light of the room.

During their talk together, the old man described to the psychiatrist his struggle to find his way around yet another strange environment; his not-too-successful attempts to adjust to unfamiliar routines and people; his loneliness, frustration, and anger; and his hostility toward the staff, whom he viewed as less than helpful or friendly. "Sometimes," he said, "they [the staff] make me do things I don't want to do. And I just don't like being pushed around." When asked about his urinating on the walls, he seemed surprised because as he pointed out, in the last place he lived, all the men used wall urinals. So, when he felt the need, he had no other choice but to use what was available, namely, the dayroom "urinals." At least that's what he thought they were. After all, the lighting was very dim and his eyesight was bad. The psychiatrist also discovered that the staff had never told this man directly what their complaints about him were. They merely vented expressions of distaste over what they called his "dirtiness" and his lack of cooperation, much to the old man's genuine bewilderment.

Following up this account, the psychiatrist contacted the institution's maintenance people and insisted that new and brighter lighting be installed in the dayroom immediately. Moreover, he insisted that the entire dayroom, including the radiators, be painted a uniform, attractive color except for the exit door. This was to be painted a bright, glowing red.

And on the corridor wall outside and opposite that door a bright red stripe was to be painted, shoulder high, all the way down the corridor leading to the men's room, as a directional cue.

All of this took some explaining and negotiating, but in about two weeks the job was done. Result: The complaining staff now began expressing their surprise, amazement, and pleasure over what they saw as a miracle cure of this man's senility on the part of the psychiatrist. Now they could report the man's cooperativeness and, what was most gratifying to them, his now finding the way to and using the men's room. You see, the staff was not wrong about the facts, but their conclusions from the facts were very much different from those of the psychiatrist. The important lesson to be learned from such an incident is that often what passes for senility may not be senility at all, but something quite different.

Are we wrong, then, to assume that an older person is not going to have the dexterity, the physical mobility, or even the nimbleness of mind of a younger one? If physical energy is the issue, we all know that the average professional baseball player is an "old man" at thirty-five. The average professional football player is "ancient" and probably expected to retire by the time he hits forty. Sports, when one is making a living at them as a professional, require the physical energy and agility of youth. The trouble with expecting sportsmen to be out of the game by age forty is that this expectation too easily gets applied to all activity and questions the capabilities of older people in general.

When it comes to mental agility, research and experience have convincingly shown us that people at seventy-seven or even eighty-seven years can be as nimble of mind as they were at forty, maybe in some respects even more so. This is another way of saying that individual IQs do not decline just because people are getting older. If IQ does decline, it is likely due to the old principle that if you don't use it, you'll lose it. If older people don't use (stimulate) their minds as they might, they may appear to lose some mental vitality. They may also appear to become more "out of it." That doesn't mean they're becoming stupid. It probably means that some of what they know is becoming obsolete. The trick of the game in helping your oldsters, then, is to help provide maximum opportunities for mental stimulation. For as people age, if they continue to be involved in intellectual exercise, not only is IQ maintained, but there is evidence it can even go up.

We are finding out that older people, while perhaps not as nimble of body as they once were, *definitely can be as nimble of mind*. Everything else being equal, in certain circumstances the older person can learn better than a younger one. With age comes experience and the older person can build upon this experience. He has the advantage of an extensive network of learning "hooks" upon which to hang some of the new information and knowledge. At the same time, this ability to add newly gained knowledge to past experience is not automatic. There is an aging process involved, and the older individual may need additional time to digest (process) the new information. You cannot in all fairness, therefore, expect the older individual to perform within the same time limits as you would expect a younger one to do. Older individuals need to pace themselves. Assuming all other processes are moving along smoothly, and there are no major mental or physical impairments, there is no doubt that old dogs can indeed be taught new tricks!

This doesn't mean that you won't find some older persons who will stubbornly cling to old points of view and resist new learning. Because of this resistance, the myth has arisen that growing old means becoming more rigid. However, in contrast to this, for example, research done in Israel has shown that some of the elderly immigrants were often more receptive to new ideas than were some of the native born, the young Sabras. This provides some evidence that a person's unwillingness to accept new ideas is not necessarily a product of old age. Even the young can be unreceptive, unwilling to absorb new information. Clinging to old ideas or resisting new ones may have to do with an individual life-style, or it may be the result of the way in which information is presented. Under certain favorable circumstances an older person may be less rigid and more amenable to creative solutions and more open to new ideas than a younger person because he (the older one), with his greater backlog of experience, may be less apprehensive or threatened by innovation.

An honest answer to the question, What is senility? is that no one, including professionals and experts, really can define clearly what senility is. In any event, senilelike behavior is not the true face of old age. Very often it is a mask that can deceive you about what is going on with your oldster.

Professionals and experts do know that certain conditions (some physical, some environmental, some emotional) can, and apparently do, cause some of those behaviors that we label as senility. One very common and apparent cause is damage to the brain cells, which can result when an insufficient supply of oxygen reaches the cells. This occurs, for example, in instances where capillaries that feed brain cells fail. Such an occurrence is referred to as a cerebral-vascular accident (CVA), or stroke. The affected brain cells die and, once dead, are never replaced.

Brain damage is likely to affect behavior initially by causing some confusion or memory lapses. But overall, behavior that results from brain damage may be due to several possibilities. Simply to assume, because of memory losses, that senility has set in can be a dreadful mistake. For instance, how often have you looked for a particular item and not been able to find it? Later you find it and realize it was merely misplaced; you had forgotten where you put it. Would this behavior mean senility if you were eighty or ninety years of age?

The fact is that as many people age, they do have the experience of memory becoming more like a fishnet with large holes than a fine screen. In other words, more information seems to slip through. And undoubtedly your older person may, under certain circumstances, show signs of disorientation or confusion. This could be (but is not necessarily) the result of brain damage. If the damage is slight and involves only a tiny area of the brain, the event may pass practically unnoticed, even by the one to whom it's happening.

Strokes are one source of brain damage. If you should happen to be present while a tiny stroke is taking place, you might see nothing more dramatic than a momentary "freezing" of the person's posture, perhaps a momentary confusion—and nothing more. At the other extreme, a massive stroke can cause paralysis. Strokes can also cause loss of ability to speak understandably or cause loss of ability to comprehend when being spoken to. Strokes can sometimes even lead to death. But in between these two extremes, there are many variations and gradations of behavior resulting from a stroke. These can include some degree of confusion.

Take the term *confusion*, which can be a very slippery word indeed. Many times those who use it or write about it do not make clear what kind of confusion they are referring to. And there are different kinds of confusion. I am thinking, as an example (and it is not an uncommon one), of an elderly individual living in a retirement or nursing home who happens to say to a staff person one day, "I'm having trouble finding my room." If this happens several times a week, most likely that individual will be called confused—and correctly so. But that doesn't go far enough! We must go on to ask, Confused with respect to what? And why? Obviously in this instance the oldster was having great difficulty locating his or her room. And that's being confused. But even though that person might be having trouble finding his room, he may still be quite capable of remembering his own name, the names of relatives, the time of day or date, and other pertinent things. Clearly, a person can be confused about some things and not confused at all about others, all at the same time.

In a way, the situation may be very much like moving into a new neighborhood. You know your own name, you haven't forgotten members of your family, you know the city, but for about the first six months you keep getting lost in your new neighborhood. Quite clearly this kind of confusion is substantially different from mental derangement or incompetence. It has much more to do with the degree of familiarity with circumstances, with the number of times you have had the chance to make your way through the area, and so on. To understand better the behavior of your oldster, you need to examine the facts and see what they mean in a particular instance. Just taken by itself, being confused about a certain specific thing, especially when the circumstances warrant it, is a long, long road from senility.

When brain damage does occur, the label given to such an event is the general term *organic brain syndrome* (OBS). When it first occurs, it's called acute brain syndrome. If damage to the brain and behavior associated with it appear to be of long standing or have not changed through treatment, it is labeled "chronic brain syndrome" (CBS). Our immediate concern with this is that so-called acute brain syndrome is usually described as treatable or reversible, or at least potentially so. Chronic brain syndrome, on the other hand, is invariably viewed as irreversible and therefore incurable. The victim, for all practical purposes, is written off.

The fact is that when first attempting to evaluate a situation, it's very difficult to tell the difference between acute and chronic brain syndrome without a very careful, conscientious investigation and evaluation of the individual's physical condition. That's why a thorough physical assessment by an experienced, patient, and understanding physician is a very important first step. Such an examination may reveal evidence of brain damage. Brain damage is no more reversible than age itself is reversible. *But what may very well be reversible is the behavior or disability associated with the brain damage.*

Some senilelike behavior (for example, memory lapses) may indeed be caused by brain damage. Some kinds of vision loss cannot be cured by medicine, surgery, or exercise. But the poor vision that accompanies the physical condition can be "cured" or corrected by the simple device of wearing glasses; with them you can function as if you had 20/20 vision. The same can be said of hearing loss. The physical condition may not be treatable or reversible, but an appropriately fitted hearing aid (which, like glasses, is a prosthetic device) can enable one to function as if with good natural hearing.

When memory slippage (it should really not be called memory loss; almost always *some* memory is retained) occurs because of (perhaps) a stroke, damage from the stroke cannot be changed. But it may be possible to do something helpful about the memory slippage that accompanies the stroke: things like memory retraining, perhaps, or encouraging the individual to write himself reminder notes, or making use of other reminders and cues (the way we use the buzzers and lights to remind us to use the seat belts and release the hand brakes of our autos). Perhaps we need to ask absentminded professors how they manage!

Brain damage means that some part of the brain, perhaps only a very small part of it, no longer functions. How much this affects the individual's ability to get along efficiently depends upon which part of the brain is affected and upon how severe and extensive the damage is. If a very tiny part of the brain is affected, the ability to function is probably not severely hampered. On the other hand, a great deal of damage, as in a series of massive strokes, can do a great deal of harm.

If such damage is noticed early, there can be retraining. For example, the damage may occur in the area where speech is affected. A good therapist, if brought into the picture early, can begin retraining a person to speak intelligibly and in some instances almost perfectly again. Recouping is also possible for stroke victims who are left with a partial paralysis following the attack. Through retraining, if started early enough, individuals can learn to function again almost to full capacity. What happens in effect is that another part of the brain takes over for the damaged part.

The only way one can judge the effectiveness of retraining with stroke victims is to look very carefully at whether the treatment used is appropriate and the most effective that can be used. Where stroke victims do not respond or seem not to respond, the nub of the matter may be that the wrong treatment is being used —or for that matter, no real "treatment" at all. Note the repeated reference here to the condition "if started early enough." That's the key to success. Retraining should ideally begin within a week—or even a few days—of the occurrence of a stroke. The longer you wait, the less likely that the treatment will be effective.

Damage to the brain, however, is certainly not the sole cause of senilelike behavior. There are many other nonphysical events that contribute to or may even trigger behaviors that we often call senile. Still another possibility is that other events may exaggerate the effects of even a very small amount of brain damage already present. For example, if the living environment of any person is so ambiguous, confusing, or complicated as to make too many demands upon him, he can—and probably will—begin to show signs of the confusion or disorientation that we usually associate with senility. This is especially apt to happen if that older individual is already experiencing much screening out of the world because of the accumulation of many sensory losses.

That is not the only cause for such behavior. Reliable evidence supports the notion that if an older person is treated persistently in a patronizing manner (as if he were a not-too-bright child), if options are removed by others who take complete control, if the person is continually demeaned and belittled and treated coldly and with indifference (whether that happens quite openly or very subtly), you can bet that some senilelike behavior is likely to occur. Some oldsters will strongly resist this kind of treatment; some will even fight back! But others will not; they will simply begin to lapse into senile behavior. In other words, if middle-agers treat their elderly parents as if they were entering a second childhood, you'll most likely see in such cases the working out of a self-fulfilling prophecy. Don't be surprised if your elderly begin to act exactly the way you treat them!

You can't fully understand the needs of your own elders, and therefore you're not likely to respond appropriately to their needs, until you take into account their personal, emotional reactions to their own life experiences. As multiple losses begin to accumulate, old Uncle Charlie becomes increasingly aware of this state of affairs. He becomes very sensitive to how impairments and disabilities can interfere with the level of competence he previously had. This awareness usually generates an enormous feeling of loss and vulnerability. Often this quite natural emotional reaction tends to exaggerate even minor losses.

More than anything else, we need to be terribly sensitive to the tremendous traumatic impact upon an already emotionally vulnerable person when he hears thoughtless remarks by family or friends about how he is "fading" or how his "mind is slipping" or how he is "not as he used to be" and the like.

The degree of embarrassment and chagrin of an older person can hardly be exaggerated when food spilled by a trembling hand or an accident of incontinence draws a thoughtless comment. The embarrassment is even more intense when comments are made publicly in front of the older person as if he were not present or can't hear—or if he can hear, as if he is unable to comprehend what is being said. Let's look at some case histories.

Mrs. X was a tall, attractive, silver-haired woman in her mid-seventies whom I had been seeing in my private practice on a weekly basis. She was an alert, intelligent widow whose husband had left her quite well-off financially. She worked at a volunteer job she liked and had a good relationship with her son and his family, whom she visited weekly. She entered my office one afternoon, obviously deeply troubled, with the startling announcement, "I think I'm losing my mind."

Her routine upon returning each afternoon from her volunteer job was to fix herself a drink and then watch TV while sipping it. In recent weeks she had begun to notice, she said, that she couldn't for the life of her remember that evening or the next day what she had been watching earlier on TV. She described these memory lapses as "blackouts."

Discussion made it clear that Mrs. X's memory for other events appeared quite intact. Why, then, these blackouts, or lapses? When it became apparent that Mrs. X turned on the TV only to get some companionable noise in the room and that she had no real investment or personal interest in the program, it also became clear that Mrs. X was barely paying attention to the TV programs that she was watching without really seeing.

Now that's a common enough experience. So is, for example, looking at a book while preoccupied with other thoughts and not really seeing the page, or being engrossed in conversation with a passenger in a car and not paying attention to streets or neighborhoods or directions. And we all know how impossible it is later to recall the TV program or the printed word or directions for getting across town. So with Mrs. X. Obviously she was not losing her mind even though that's what at first her memory lapse meant to her.

Most important of all in this discussion with Mrs. X was the intense fright and feeling of apprehension that gripped her at the thought (as she at first saw it) that she was losing her mind. Her realization that she had not been very interested or involved in the TV, and that this explained her blackouts, effectively eliminated her fears.

In another case, a middle-aged woman called to make an appointment for her mother, Mrs. Y, a woman in her late sixties. She was fearful that her mother (Mrs. Y) might be "going senile." The evidence? Over the past year, Mrs. Y had been having difficulty in sleeping (had taken to tranquilizers), was growing increasingly restless and nervous, had trouble with her appetite, frequently forgot familiar names, and had trouble keeping track of calendar dates. This seemed especially distressing to a daughter who characterized her mother as having "always been a very calm, extremely easygoing, relaxed kind of person," who was very bright and always "on top" of things.

Mother and daughter came in together and related these facts: Mrs. Y, a widow, had been living in a retirement home for the past five years, where she had become very much involved with the activities and organizational life of the residents. They had organized a club and for about four years Mrs. Y served as the secretary-treasurer, a position she loved because there weren't too many members at first and so keeping the books was a fairly simple matter. Besides, she had worked as a bookkeeper some years back, and now she felt involved, needed, useful, and worthwhile. Over the past year or so, however, the membership had grown by leaps and bounds. Demands upon her time and energies were more than she had reckoned with; she was having trouble keeping track of the membership and thus began to experience the symptoms mentioned above.

In sheer desperation the daughter finally persuaded Mrs. Y to consult her physician, and through him arrangements were made for Mrs. Y to enter a hospital, where she remained for about ten days while extensive tests and observations were completed. The result? An absolutely clean bill of health. Following the tests, Mrs. Y came to spend a few days in her daughter's home, and it was then that I was contacted.

It was immediately apparent that the daughter, without being aware of it, was subtly reinforcing some deep, underlying fear or apprehension in her mother.

We explored at length the matter of her memory lapses. As might be expected, occasional forgetting was certainly no new experience for Mother. We also talked about the growing pressures of her secretary-treasurer job and what it was like to begin to feel overwhelmed by its demands. We discussed her fear of being unable to keep up or to measure up, her growing resentment at the bind she found herself in, and finally how all these things had begun to add up to nervousness and sleeplessness and all her other symptoms.

But there was still the preoccupation of both mother and daughter with the memory lapses, the forgetting. And so when I finally mentioned the word *senility*, both women for the first time looked truly frightened. Quite clearly, the underlying fear in both mother and daughter was that all the symptoms signified to them the first signs of senility. And that meant to them the beginning of the end.

What was most certainly called for was a considerable amount of reassurance about this, and providing just that made a happy outcome possible. The reassurance consisted in getting them both to see that Mother's symptoms could easily be accounted for on the basis of the stress she had been encountering. In other words, her memory lapses did not indicate that catastrophe lay just over the horizon. The happy outcome was evident in mother's and daughter's expressed sense of relief, which enabled them to go on to deal directly with the sources of the stress.

The point is, in observing certain events that puzzle, distress, mystify, or even annoy you, what you do next or how you respond will pretty much depend upon what those observed facts mean to you. Those facts may not be the only facts that you must take into account. Such things may have quite different causes than you think. To jump to the conclusion (at the appearance of strange or unusual behaviors) that a state of senility has set in (and irreversible, at that!) may indeed be a grave injustice inflicted upon the older person you care for.

Senilelike behavior can also be caused by certain disease processes as well as by other conditions that themselves are treatable and curable. This is usually the case, for instance, with such conditions as anemia, monoxide poisoning, an inadequate supply of thiamine or nicotinic acid, and toxicity, to name a few. Ordinarily such diseases or conditions are treatable and curable if steps are taken before more permanent damage takes place. It's not a rare occurrence for a physician to diagnose an elderly person as senile when in reality the underlying cause may be one of these treatable conditions.

We are also coming to realize that too many aged persons are misdiagnosed as senile when they are merely depressed over some life circumstance. And others, as they age, seem to change behavior. My own bias is that every event has some reason for its occurrence, even if we can't immediately discover what that reason might be. Thus, when middle-aged sons and daughters describe their bewilderment at "sudden" personality changes in their elderly, a strong word of caution is needed. That word of caution is twofold: (1) behavior doesn't happen in a vacuum, nor does it happen for no reason at all; and (2) there is a well-established principle of human behavior that refers to the consistency of personality across the life span into the later years.

We cannot escape the fact that each of us is heir to his own history. The fruit of our lives in the later years doesn't fall very far from the main branch of our life's cycle. Simply translated, the person who is warm, loving, and considerate through his early and middle years is likely to be as warm, loving, and considerate a person in the later years of life. By the same token, take the cranky, irritable, self-centered old man or woman. If you looked at that individual thirty years before, you're likely to see a person with pretty much the same characteristics. Psychological study has made a pretty good case for what we might call the consistency of personality throughout the life span.

There might be an instance where an elderly mother who has always been known by her family to be a neat, almost compulsively clean, housekeeper, "suddenly" seems to give it all up. The family is not only disturbed but shocked to see how slovenly she has become about her personal appearance and how she has let things get grubby, even dirty, with dirty dishes in the sink for days, papers on the floor, and so on, in a house or apartment that she used to keep spick-and-span. What's gone wrong?

Or take the case of an elderly lady who always was identified by her relatives and friends as a quiet, compliant, unassertive housewife who "knew her place." She now "suddenly" appears to have changed character! She has become a domineering, aggressive master over her now passive husband and seems to have taken over complete control of the household.

To come to any true understanding of these circumstances, it's necessary to look beyond the immediate events described and examine very carefully the life-style of such individuals over the years. By so doing, it's not unusual to discover that those sudden personality changes or those unexpected out-of-character behaviors may not be novel at all. They may have been there right along, only they were masked by circumstances. Now, when life circumstances have changed, the old characteristics are merely uncovered and come to the surface. The family is really seeing them unadorned for the first time.

Let's go back to the example of the compulsive housekeeper. It may well be that this woman always hated housework right from the beginning of her marriage. But "women's lib" had not yet appeared on the scene, and she was raised to believe that her prime obligation and duty as a housewife was to keep an orderly and clean house. Thus she fulfilled her duty over the years. But now circumstances have changed. Her children are grown and out of the house, there are very few visitors, and she has much less incentive left, to say nothing of energy, to induce her to carry on an activity she has really always disliked—and so she lets the housecleaning go. And maybe personal grooming gets neglected along the way too. Given this understanding of those events, don't we find ourselves empathizing a little more with this woman? And don't we find our hearts going out to her a bit more?

And the second example. This woman may have been aggressive and domineering all along. But these characteristics went relatively unnoticed because most of her energy was spent on controlling her children (when everyone put that in the context of child-rearing), servants, and tradespeople. Her husband wasn't around very much of the time, so he didn't notice either. Now circumstances have changed in her life too. Her husband is retired and at home a lot and he has become much more passive. There are no children around to siphon off her energies. And not least of all, she is no longer content to keep in "her place" (which always did imply inferior status). And so "suddenly" she is seen as aggressive and domineering, traits that are at last coming to the surface.

By this time you ought to have a little better idea of how to come to terms with the issue of senilelike behavior in your aged folks. The very first injunction to you is this: Don't panic! Keep in mind it is worth the effort to get a more precise appraisal of your dear elderly. Your responsibility is to try to understand fully what's happening before prematurely labeling them as "senile." Such labeling may be based on misinformation or too little information. In that case, you get locked into the position that nothing can be done for them except minimal caretaking: provide a clean bed to sleep on, three adequate meals a day (plus snacks), some medication, an occasional patronizing pat on the head, and beyond that, not much of anything. That's the kiss of death for them, psychologically. When that occurs, physical deterioration cannot be far behind.

We need to be very sensitive to the implications of events and ask ourselves what they really mean. Then we must decide how we are going to respond to them with accurate empathy, common sense, fairness, and a humane respect for individuality.

3

Does Growing Old Mean Dropping Out?

INDIVIDUAL EXPERIENCE OF AGE IS UNIQUE. . . .
LONELINESS, THE BANE OF OLD AGE. . . . BECOMING A
SOCIAL DROPOUT IS NOT INEVITABLE. . . . OBSTACLES TO
SOCIAL CONTACTS. . . . SPECIAL VULNERABILITY OF THE
ELDERLY. . . . GREATEST BARRIER TO SEX AMONG THE
AGED. . . . ADAPTATION TO PHYSICAL CHANGE. . . . KNOW
YOUR ELDERLY PARENT AS A PERSON.

Everything we observe and hear about old age from those who have gone through or are going through the process tells us that the most important consideration is the way one experiences the process. In the very same way that there is an enormous variety of meanings that you as an individual attach to your own early memories of the experiences of your childhood, adolescence, and young adulthood, there is an infinite difference in the ways individuals experience old age.

No one knows what being seventy-five years old is supposed to feel like, and only those who get there know what it is like. One thing is sure—it's different in at least some respects for each individual. Nonetheless, there are common experiences that are shared by many because such events are embedded in the very nature of human existence. One such common experience of aging in our society is the increased vulnerability to the effects of change and with it the increasing need to depend a little more than before on others. But loneliness is acknowledged by everyone to be one of the commonest complaints of elderly people.

Unfortunately, one of the prices we pay for surviving into the seventh, eight, and ninth decades of life and beyond is that, in most instances, those we have grown up with are gone. Friends and relatives are removed by death or lost because of relocation. Sometimes it's because of diversion of interests; family members or friends simply drift apart. In any case, family bonds are broken, and the familiar ties of friendship begin to loosen. This doesn't happen only to the elderly. But when such disruptions are added to many other losses and come at a time in life when other opportunities for adventure seem to be disappearing, you can understand what an especially heavy burden the lack of old friends and family becomes in old age. You can also begin to appreciate why many older persons, even though other things may seem to be all right, begin to become very vulnerable to loneliness.

How to cope with this loneliness is, of course, very important. The commonsense "cure," obviously, is the right contacts with people, just as the cure for poverty is money and the cure for boredom is something interesting to do. If you care a great deal about an older person, the loneliness of that person is naturally of great concern to you. It goes almost without saying that you can't live a life for anyone else. Nevertheless, you may very well be able to help reestablish some of the broken family, friendship, and other affectional bonds and ties. You can't, of course, give back a dead parent, spouse, or relative, but perhaps you can help the process of renewing old relationships or establishing new ones that can, to a great extent, compensate for the heavy losses that have such severe emotional consequences.

How an older person will respond to help in repairing the social bonds will depend upon the individual, of course. It will depend as well upon incentive, opportunity, and circumstances. Consider the following situations in the light of the notion of vulnerability to change. You've seen older persons sitting in a private home or in a retirement residence or a nursing home, lonely and isolated. Is that an inevitable accompaniment of old age—one that cannot be avoided and about which nothing can be done? For many years, a widely discussed theory about aging (known as the disengagement theory) has maintained that there is a mutual letting go on the part of both the older person and society. Elderly people have fewer social contacts with others, it was theorized, because in effect they are preparing for the "end" by gradually letting go of their network of attachments. But if we look at individual lives and particular circumstances, armed with a better knowledge of the facts, we often discover that these links with others are not necessarily being dropped because of some automatic compulsion within the individual. We discover that some older people become social dropouts for other very practical reasons.

It's usually no good simply to exhort someone to "get in touch" or "go out and make new friends" if it's not reasonably convenient, easy, and comfortable for them to do so. It's not always easy for Grandma to maintain friendships or social contacts with those who have moved away, even if it's only to the other side of town, especially if she can't afford to maintain an auto in her garage or doesn't drive. Just think of the obstacles if public transportation is not available or, if available, is much too expensive for someone on a very limited income. Then, too, you must consider that public transportation may be available and inexpensive enough but not very convenient. Just imagine what it's like for a person whose body is not as strong as it once was to face the prospect, in using public transportation (even for shopping), of having to walk five or six or more blocks and then wait a half hour for a bus or streetcar, and then to think about having to make another transfer or two to get to the final destination. Think of the prospect of having the hour-or-two process all over again on the return trip! Or think what it's like for an elderly person to have to contemplate walking down numerous flights of badly lit stairs to negotiate a subway or rapid transit system —even if it's available and cheap!

Indeed, if you want to help, you need to be sensitive to the sense of vulnerability that many older persons feel about all this but often don't put into words. Many become terribly apprehensive about all those "terrible" things they've heard can happen when they leave a relatively safe, familiar, supportive environment to venture out. Can you imagine what it's like to realize that you can't move as quickly as you once did, that your hearing and sight are not as acute as they once were, that you don't feel as steady on your feet as before, and that you don't have as much energy and stamina? What is it like to face noisy and confusing traffic; crowded buses that lurch and have high steps that make getting on and off difficult at best; the possibility of being knocked off your feet by hurrying, unheeding crowds; being fearful of forgetting where you want to go or how to get there; or having to stand on your feet for long periods of time waiting? If you are elderly and you've heard about these obstacles and hazards (often the inflamed imagination is worse than the realities), your apprehensions are not going to be reduced when you repeatedly run into warnings and dire cautions from well-intentioned family, who constantly harp on the dangers and the risks to life and limb. All these considerations are links in a chain of events that can contribute very powerfully to a loosening of social contacts or a lessening of inclination to maintain old ones or establish and develop new ones. This is when much encouragement and reassurance can make a difference to your elder, and your suggestion that he carry a little reminder note or a little map can help tremendously.

Obviously, too, some important modifications in our public transportation systems would go a long way in making increased mobility for the elderly a pleasant adventure instead of a discouraging, even terrifying, risk to life and limb. There's no doubt that more available, accessible, and cheap transportation will go a long way in supporting older persons in their efforts to maintain social contacts. Nor is there any doubt that the telephone, if available and cheap, provides much more than just a basic lifeline for emergency help. For very much the same reasons, we're at long last beginning to recognize the value and usefulness of multiservice centers and day activity programs in places throughout the community as much needed gathering places and social centers for older persons.

The apprehensions of many older persons stem from a sense of vulnerability caused by their multiple losses, of which they are acutely conscious in a way that others are not. An example of this is the case of a widow in her late seventies who came to me for counseling. Financially well-fixed, she was active in a volunteer job she loved. She enjoyed good health and an excellent relationship with her two middle-aged children and their families, whom she visited in turn on Friday and Saturday nights.

During the course of our sessions, however, she mentioned her intention of cutting down on those cherished visits to her children and grandchildren. This is what was bothering her. When visiting in their homes and sitting in a position where a member of the family was facing the other way, she began to realize how much difficulty she was having in hearing what was said and in following the conversation. She would only miss a few words here and there, but this seemed enough to cause her considerable embarrassment—either from her failure at times to respond at all or from finding out she was giving an inappropriate response to the conversation.

She hadn't failed to notice the occasional exchange of knowing looks between members of the family. She was certain that they thought she was getting a little soft in the head, maybe a bit senile. She knew she should ask the members of her family circle to speak a bit louder or to repeat the missed word or sentence for her benefit. But she was a proud, sensitive lady and found herself too chagrined and embarrassed to bring herself to ask the favor. So her solution to the problem (and not an uncommon one for many elderly) was to make polite excuses for not coming over to visit and thus gradually eliminate herself from the social situation that caused her difficulty and distress. It's the kind of solution that invariably leads to a vicious circle of increasing isolation, distance, and loss of social contact. An alternative solution, as in this instance, is to persuade such a person of the real service she would do her family and herself by asking them to speak distinctly and while facing her.

The root of social isolation in instances like this one quite plainly is not senility. The problem in this case was a moderate loss of hearing in a woman too proud to admit and do something constructive about it. Most often when such a problem is faced and recognized for what it is, a properly fitted hearing aid can make all the difference. The key phrase here is "properly fitted." Professional help should be sought because a poorly fitted aid can do more harm than good; indeed, some hearing losses or deficits within certain ranges are really not helped at all by hearing aids. It's important to know when that's the case. Certainly you wouldn't want to foreclose the possibility of future help because of the disenchantment of your elderly parent with a hearing aid that was not right for him.

An interesting observation concerning the matter of social conversation is that many older people have pointed out that at times they can understand the speech of women better than that of men, especially when face to face. I often wondered about this until I learned the reason given. It's because women wear bright lipstick that outlines the lips and makes it easier to see the lips move and figure out the words. It is very much akin to lipreading, no doubt. When carrying on a conversation with elderly persons, we ought to be sensitive to at least the possibility that their hearing might not be as acute as it could be. It is helpful whenever possible to talk face to face so that your facial expressions and the movement of your lips can easily be seen. And it's better to converse in bright light than in dim light.

On the other hand, you should never assume (as many people seem to do almost automatically) that an individual with bad eyesight must also at the same time be hard-of-hearing. Have you ever noticed how frequently people talking to the blind tend to speak in a loud tone, as if the "seeing bone" were connected to the "hearing bone." It really never hurts another's feelings to ask if you are talking clearly enough—if it's not done in a patronizing way.

The so-called extended family we were familiar with a couple of generations ago is probably gone forever because of our highly mobile society. Much more frequently than in the past, young adults and middle-aged children move from one part of the country to another because of job, career, or educational considerations, and this removes them from the primary family unit and from their older relatives. On the other hand, more and more we find older persons themselves moving to warmer, more favorable climates and in this way removing themselves from their accustomed social circles. It should be noted, however, that contrary to the usual impression, the majority of elderly parents in our society still manage to maintain fairly regular contacts with their middle-aged children, and vice versa. The notion that most elderly are abandoned by their children is strictly a myth. It does sometimes happen, sad to say, and usually because of a history of bad relationships.

But according to the surveys, it doesn't happen frequently.

There is still another circumstance that contributes to the disruption of the family or friendship network. This is a factor that has only recently begun to show itself in our culture, namely, the growing number of divorces among middle-aged and older couples. In our present society, unlike that of the past, couples who don't get along together as partners find a lot of encouragement to resolve the situation by getting a divorce. At the very minimum, society does not actively discourage such action. Nor are people generally as openly disapproving as was the case a couple of generations ago. Often many of those who divorce do not remarry, especially if they are in their middle years. Thus, more people move into the later years as singles, which, in turn, increases the possibility of loss of social contacts and loneliness in the later years.

Some older persons say in moments of candor that one of the things they miss most is the touching, the physical closeness experienced in their younger years. They genuinely miss the caresses, the warm embraces of sincere affection that nourish the heart and spirit as nothing else can. This kind of touching is the tender, loving touching that is so very personal, in contrast to a kind of "administrative" touching that takes place when you touch a person with the tips of the fingers to direct him somewhere, help him out of a wheelchair, or guide him to the table. That kind of coldly clinical touching is very different from tender touching—and just about everybody recognizes the difference!

We are all essentially social beings; therefore, we are talking about a universal need. Right from birth, it has to do with the need for closeness, for human warmth, for human responsiveness, for intimacy. It's a need that extends into the later years and, if anything, becomes more intense then. Sexuality is one of the ways in which this need for human closeness, warmth, and intimacy is expressed and fulfilled. If the need for affection on its many levels is common to us all, and few would deny it, what gets in the way of fulfilling this need in the later years of life?

As much as anything, it boils down to the general attitudes of society, particularly those of middle-agers. One thing we can't help noticing, if we pay close attention, is the reluctance on the part of many people to get physically close to the elderly. Is it the gray hair, the wrinkles, or some of the other accompanying physical changes that turn off a lot of younger people? Perhaps it may be because in our culture we are conditioned to put such a premium not only on acting youthful but also on looking youthful, and what we set as standards of beauty or attractiveness generally excludes wrinkles; liver spots; thinning, graying hair; and slowed movements. But that may only be part of the explanation. Perhaps many who are not old are reluctant to touch the old because they see the old as "different" in much the same way they see the crippled, the maimed, the blind, the sick, the retarded, the criminal, and the dispossessed as "different." And if different, then strange, alien. If alien, then distasteful. And it's difficult to draw close and touch the distasteful. But is your elder different (or alien or distasteful) just because he or she has become old?

If you're a bit skeptical about the need for affectionate touching, try this sometime with an elderly person who has very bad eyesight, bad hearing, or who seems unresponsive or "out of touch." Instead of speaking very loudly to that individual to get his attention, simply take one of his or her hands and enclose it fully and warmly in both of yours (not just the fingertips—make it close contact, palm to palm, and cover it). Wait a few moments to see what happens. You'll probably be quite surprised at the reaction, even if you do nothing more than hold his hand in that way and smile. By the same token, you'll also get a good grasp on what miracles of communication can occur when, for example, you gently and tenderly massage the naked shoulders or back of that oldster who appears to be out of touch.

From time to time, I've heard middle-agers or younger persons (especially professional helpers) describe an occasion when they've tried this approach, only to be disappointed and to feel rejected. The older individual seemed at first to be startled, then drew back, and finally shrugged off the touching hand. If that experience should ever be yours, my earnest advice is, "For goodness sake, don't give up!" More than likely that person has simply gotten unused to tender touching. Or because of past experience he may be so leery of touching that he misinterprets the overture— at first. But by all means keep it up! Start slowly, be persistent and consistent, and above all, tender. Your success in gaining a warm response is a foregone conclusion.

In addition to the affectionate gesture, the varied delights of sexual caressing and intercourse remain a potent force for pleasurable stimulation in the later years. This is a very individual matter that varies from person to person. Thanks mainly to research by people like Masters and Johnson, we have begun to learn and are only just beginning to acknowledge candidly that people do not necessarily lose their interest in affection and sexual activity just because they have reached seventy, eighty, or more years. Little by little, we are seeing the prohibitions and constraints against physical intimacy and sexual activity in old age being done away with. We are witnessing a radical change in the widespread attitude that such things are inappropriate to the later years of life. A new and better attitude is beginning to develop, although it is not nearly as widely accepted as it must and will be.

We must face the fact, as a perceptive colleague of mine has observed, that we almost never see a double bed in a nursing home. Couples who have been together for thirty or forty years or longer are separated and deprived of the comfort of each other's (or someone's!) closeness. We are still struggling with contradictory attitudes that accept sexual desire or a reaching out for physical intimacy in the young as normal but stigmatize the same behavior in the old as "lechery."

All other things being equal, people do not lose their appetite for sex as they get older. But you must keep in mind that sex, like eating, takes on a lot of symbolic meanings and is very much influenced by individual life-styles and tastes. Thus, a person who has engaged in a low or moderate level of sexual activity in his early or middle years is very likely to engage in sexual activity (including physical intimacy, closeness) at a low or moderate level in his later years. And, persons who engaged in sexual activity at a rather high level in their early and middle years are likely to continue in that manner in their later years.

One circumstance that might diminish such activity is physical illness. A second would be lack of an available, willing partner. But if you stop to think of it, these factors most likely would account for a lessening of sexual activity at any age, be it seventeen, twenty-five, or forty-three. And we are finding that, just as at any age, a great many older persons indulge in sexual activity in a solitary manner, through masturbation, simply because they do not have an available, willing partner. While the lack of a partner to share intimacy is a problem generally in the later years, it is more acute among older women in our society because women tend to outlive men in significant proportions, something on the order of about five or six to one. Thus, after sixty or seventy years of age, we have a much larger proportion of the older population who are women and widowed, while there is a smaller population of older males, and they are, for the most part, married and thus unavailable to the single widows.

Assuming the availability of older men and women, what difficulties are to be faced in seeking intimate relationships? Your elderly might indeed be looking around for a compatible partner, somebody who will meet the need for intimacy. What happens if the relationship develops beyond friendship into the need for sexual expression? Imagine what it's like if you and other people around them respond in a manner that implies they are being silly, or not acting their age? How many of us still believe sex is only for the young? If we do, the older person, faced with this sort of reaction, is surely going to be inhibited from pursuing the kind of closeness and the intimacy he or she wants to share.

And, of course, older people, through years of conditioning, may themselves take the view that sex in the later years is somehow inappropriate, silly, or just not the right thing to do. All of this, our attitudes and those produced in older people through the years, can discourage men and women in their later years from seeking partners for their very legitimate sexual needs. We ought not encourage such an attitude; on the other hand, the moral or ethical constraints and beliefs of the individual need to be respected.

We know that, generally speaking, in the later years some reduction in the amount of available energy begins to take place. Along with this we know that it begins to take a little longer for a male to achieve an erection, and women find that it takes a little more time for the vagina to lubricate. Sometimes for older women, therefore, intercourse may initially be a little bit uncomfortable. In such an instance, women should be encouraged to use all the help they can get. An understanding family physician, for example, can suggest an appropriate lubricating cream. Nevertheless, this has nothing whatsoever to do with the ability to have intercourse or the full capability of enjoying it. What also is required is more loving foreplay, stroking, patience, and understanding on the part of both partners. But that need be no burden to an older couple. Isn't that a desirable ingredient of sexuality at any age?

Being unaware of the changes accompanying old age can cause a considerable amount of misunderstanding, anxiety, and distress. It can even cause malfunction. So it was with a couple in their seventies, married for over forty years, who came to me for counseling. What was gnawing at the heart of the woman was a dawning conviction that her husband no longer cared for her as he had in the past. When I asked why she felt that way, she rather reluctantly explained that she had noticed for some months when they were together in the bedroom particularly for the purpose of making love and she took her clothes off, he did not respond with an erection as quickly as she had known him to do previously. From this she had begun to conclude, to her great distress, that she was losing her appeal for him and that his affection for her was ebbing.

What she most needed was the assurance that certain expected physiological changes were taking place and if they were both aware of this and prepared to give each other a little more time, additional caresses, added strokes, and some extra stimulation, all other things being equal, they would find the twin fires of affection and desire still burning, steady and warm.

There must be the recognition of some slowing down, some diminishing of energy with the added years, and the willingness on the part of both partners to provide enough stimulation and time for the natural physical response to take place. Because of the delay in response associated with age, it should certainly not be concluded that one partner cares less for the other. In addition, there are other possible sources of stress, other circumstances that may prove to be obstacles. Impotence in an elderly male (or its counterpart in the female, frigidity) is not something he likes to talk about. But it does happen (though *not* because of aging) and what is more important, it can almost invariably be successfully treated and cured.

I am thinking of a man in his middle sixties who was left a widower after thirty years of a very good marriage. He had to struggle mightily to retain his emotional equilibrium under the enormous impact of his loss and the wrenching grief he felt. He also had to wrestle with the not inconsiderable adjustments of living alone after so many years of companionship.

He had a neighbor, an attractive widow in her fifties, who knew his situation and was extremely sympathetic. Shortly after the funeral of his wife she began bringing in an occasional casserole for her neighbor, which he very much appreciated. He especially welcomed the chance to talk to someone. In time they began to dine together and share some wine. Finally, one evening, these two lonely people came together in her house, in her bedroom.

But the occasion turned out to be less delightful and idyllic than it might have been. In the course of much tender caressing, this man became acutely self-conscious of his being, for the first time in thirty years, in an intimate situation with a woman other than his wife. In addition, he happened to be in his neighbor's bedroom, a very strange place for him. He was still struggling with his grief over his loss; this was a strange woman and he was in an unfamiliar role. And besides all that, he had really had a little too much wine to drink that night. All of this added up to his inability to get an erection, which caused much disappointment and consternation on the part of both. Moreover, he couldn't really understand why this had happened.

Not surprisingly, when the opportunity and the invitation for another encounter with this attractive lady took place a week or so later, this man began to experience nagging doubts and apprehensions about his own adequacy, and thus the stage was set for a self-fulfilling prophecy. His nagging fear that he might not do well or perform sexually almost guaranteed the anticipated failure.

The point is that the outcome as described was not at all because of his age. Rather it came about from a whole series and combination of factors (which could conceivably add up to the same outcome at any age)— his being with a relative stranger in an unfamiliar place and circumstance when he was already under considerable stress. With appropriate, supportive counseling this kind of sexual problem is usually easily solved. After some discussion, reassurance, and insight on his part, this man reduced and finally eliminated his fears and anxieties. He was able to go on to full participation in the joy of sex as he had in the past.

It should be emphasized that this type of situation —this feeling of inability to perform satisfactorily—is as applicable to a woman as to a man. The very same thing can happen to a widow in strange circumstances with a man she likes and knows but where the situation is new or stressful. She might experience something like unpleasantness or even some pain at intercourse and might view this as a sign of something physically wrong with her because of her age. It really has nothing to do with that! What we are talking about is not an aging problem but a human one! Professional counseling and help can be very useful at this juncture. Even more than that, what is needed is the loving support, reassurance, and encouragement of family and friends. Your positive assistance can make all the difference as far as the continued happiness of your oldster is concerned.

When you as the middle-ager see or sense the possibility of some sexual activity on the part of your elderly mother or dad, you may (in spite of yourself) be startled or shocked because of your own attitudes or your own lingering beliefs in some myths about old age. It's not fair to say you should not be shocked or startled. But it *is* fair to say that if you genuinely care about your parent, you have no right to lay the burden of your own sense of shock or indignation on him or her. Because that makes what is really *your* problem your parent's problem.

Does growing old mean becoming a social dropout? The answer is *NO!* Or, to put it more accurately, your elderly are probably going to need your help to make it so. You can begin by identifying the needs of the older person as well as the opportunities and options that are available for reestablishing friendship networks that have been disrupted. This may not be as simple a matter as it appears at first glance.

It is still (to me) surprising and somewhat disconcerting to discover how many middle-aged sons and daughters have very little personal and intimate knowledge about their parents. It is rather rare that children have been able to know their parents from inside the skin, so to speak. Usually middle-aged offspring, when asked, describe parents in terms of their physical characteristics or their activities or their habits. Not too often do children seem to get to know their parents' hopes, dreams, fantasies, and aspirations. What may, therefore, be required of you—perhaps for the first time—is to explore and discuss with your elderly parents their hopes, dreams, aspirations, longings, new interests, goals, and the like.

We all recognize that it is impossible to give back a parent or relative who has been lost, but it is possible to compensate by helping to reestablish worthwhile friendships. One way is to provide living opportunities where your elder can be in contact with a range of people. It is known, for example, that most older people prefer to live with and socialize with people in their age group. This is not unusual because persons of any age prefer to be with their peers, their own social class, and so on. Living together in facilities such as apartment houses or other kinds of congregate living (like retirement residences) are generally preferred by most older people—that is, if they can find one congenial to their life-style.

Finding living situations for older persons with their peers is not an absolutely final answer either because many will also tell you that they just don't want to be with older people exclusively. Most don't want to be locked into what they might call an old-age ghetto. That is to say, they also would like the opportunity to mix from time to time with people of other ages. Many older people love contact with children, for instance, though usually in reasonably small doses.

What else can be arranged to keep oldsters within the framework of society? We are seeing a new social phenomenon called day activity programs or day activity centers. They are rapidly gaining popularity as society responds more to the needs of older people. They provide a place in the community where older persons can go (especially if they are not employed or are retired from any active service) and spend a good part of the day in a program of varied activities. The range of pursuits covers a broad spectrum from arts and crafts to cooking to adult education to counseling to special travel opportunities and art discussion groups.

Of course, there are some variations in these multiservice centers, but the important thing is that they are centers where people can go and do interesting things and spend their days not only in a satisfying but also productive way. They do this together with people of similar interests and in similar circumstances, so they have opportunities to develop friendships and maintain them.

In a sense these programs are a substitution for the varied activities of the extended family, which seems to be on the way out in modern society. They are a way to enable people to do something useful and interesting and to help them retreat from isolation and get back into the mainstream of productive living.

4

Retirement—
from Termination
to Transition

HAVING SOMETHING TO RETIRE TO. . . . THE SECRET OF
SUCCESSFUL RETIREMENT. . . . A BALANCE BETWEEN NEEDS
OF THE MIDDLE-AGED AND THE ELDERLY. . . . IS
RETIREMENT AN ANACHRONISM? . . . COERCION IS NOT
THE ANSWER. . . . LATE LIFE IS ALSO THE AGE OF
DISCOVERY. . . . SECOND, PARALLEL, AND ALTERNATIVE
"CAREERS" IN LATER LIFE. . . . FALSE STARTS AND SUCCESS
EXPERIENCES. . . . A NEW LOOK AT PRODUCTIVITY.

For some, retirement may represent the pot of gold at the end of the rainbow. At least that's what some people say. On the other hand, a great many more people are saying (in more ways than one) that they are neither adequately prepared for the later years of life nor are they particularly satisfied with them when they come. At that point in their lives I have seen older persons look around them with haunted eyes and say, "What do I do with the rest of my life?"

One day several years ago, a seventy-six-year-old woman sat in my office and told me in a quiet voice of nearly forty years spent in her chosen career as a nurse. The work, concerns, and struggle of those years were etched in her face, her gray hair, and her hands. But what she made so plain to me was the immense pride and inner satisfaction she felt in that lifetime investment of herself—the sense of purpose and fulfillment her career had given her. What came through quite clearly was that nursing had been much more than just a job to her. She had used her intelligence and developed and used her skills in ways that made a difference in the lives of others; she felt she had been useful, needed. Her life, at least up to that point, had been worthwhile.

About eight years prior to our meeting, she had decided she wanted a rest from an almost uninterrupted career of nursing. Her husband had been ailing and she wanted the time to stay home and care for him. She had thus retired from nursing and had taken on full time the care of her husband. Gradually, however, he began to fail, and within a two-year period he died. For several years now she had been alone. Much of her time was spent reading and making occasional excursions to her church, to markets, or to a local concert or movie. But mostly she was at loose ends, restless and bored. Even worse, she began to experience increasing anxiety over her now noticeable lapses of memory, periods of daydreaming, and episodes of depression. Having related all this to me that day, she looked at me searchingly and then remarked poignantly, almost as if to herself, "You know, the real trouble was that I had nothing to retire *to!*"

This nurse's story gives a good reason why some sensible—and early—preparing for the later years can lay the groundwork for successful aging. Early preparation can help bypass some pitfalls, avoid some disappointments, create options that then open the door to more choices, and provide more opportunity for alternatives. This is what planning for the later years is all about—preparation and involvement. I want to underscore the importance of preparing for later life on another level than merely saving money or making good investments, although that seems worthwhile in itself. Such preparation goes beyond mere economic security. There is more to it than satisfying yourself that Mother will have enough money for her old age, or that Dad will have a clean, comfortable room and bed.

The case of Mr. K, an eighty-two-year-old gentleman who came to see me with his son and daughter and their spouses, illustrates the point. The family group presented a complex set of conflicting interests. Dad was a small, wiry, industrious gentleman who had come to this country as a young boy, eventually settling in a large metropolitan area where he opened a small auto repair shop. By dint of much perseverance and by working diligently ten to twelve hours a day, six days a week, he had built his small shop into a very successful business enterprise. About eight years prior to our meeting, Mr. K's wife died. Shortly thereafter he retired, turned the business over to his son, and moved in with his daughter and son-in-law. That's when the trouble began.

Mr. K is a feisty, assertive man with a considerable amount of energy. His shop was still the center of his life, and therefore he insisted on going to work every day along with his son. Understandably, he wanted to be close to the scene of his life's success. During the hours he spent at the shop, he was more than an idle observer, as one might guess. He felt it his prerogative to comment—often critically—on the work, the skill, and the accomplishments of the employees. He frequently issued orders and sometimes even took it upon himself to fire a worker on the spot. All this in spite of the fact that ostensibly his son was the boss. Plainly, these events created a great many difficulties in running the shop and embarrassment for the son.

More than that, Dad still liked to view himself as the head of the household even though now living in his daughter and son-in-law's home. Conflict arose in that home, for instance, when Dad insisted on sitting at the head of the table, as was his custom for years in his own home. His daughter and son-in-law felt a lot of resentment, for example, when Dad would meet their invited company at the door on a Saturday night and invite them into his room for a visit and then monopolize them for the evening. This he did though the guests had come to socialize with his daughter and son-in-law. Antagonism boiled up into the open when Dad insisted on being served in his daughter's home as he was when still living with his own wife and being waited on by her as he had been throughout his married life. Things went from bad to worse, even to the point where Dad refused to speak to his son-in-law. Dad clearly was not happy, his middle-aged children even less so.

I have described this family at some length because their lives show some of the very common human conflicts that arise between the middle-aged and their elderly parents. For one thing, even though it seemed that Dad had turned the business that he had built over to his son, there was no clear-cut agreement between the two as to who the boss *really* was. Second, there was the unresolved issue as to whether Dad was to be the head of his daughter and son-in-law's home or to be an honored and welcome guest.

Two sets of interests were plainly in conflict here: the need and right of daughter and son and their spouses to live their lives, pursue their careers, and maintain their own social contacts without undue coercion or interference from their father; on the other side, the right and need of this elderly man to maintain his own sense of self-esteem and his need not to be put on the shelf (or "shuffled into a corner," as he put it).

These conflicting interests, all legitimate in themselves, needed to be sorted out and dealt with. A major difficulty in finding solutions, we began to discover, was the fact that this elderly father had in no way adequately prepared himself for his later years. When we eventually did begin to talk about other interests (other than his shop, for example), like hobbies, his response was, "Hobbies? What hobbies?" He had no hobbies, no avocational interests, no alternative to work developed over the years. He was not much of a TV-watcher, nor even a reader. His shop had been his whole life. It appeared to have been the one thing that gave meaning to his existence. To take that away seemed the equivalent of taking away his reason for living. And therein lay the dilemma.

When an older person whose life has included nothing but work faces retirement, what can be done so that the later years are not empty ones? Early preparation can go a long way toward establishing life activities that are as rewarding as work. But beyond that evident truth, you need to look at the life of your elderly from a different point of view. Instead of asking what they should do *after* retirement, perhaps you should ask yourself if there should really be any retirement for them at all, at least in the usual sense of the word.

As you think about how you might help, please consider two things. One is that it just may well be that retirement as we have known and practiced it over the years may now be an anachronism, completely out of date.

The second thing to consider is the change in interests and life goals that can come along with the later years. In the past it was customary for a man to work at a given job, in one place, for a particular boss or company, over a span of thirty-five years or so and then retire to enjoy the "golden years," that is, what few remained to him. Less and less does that appear to be the customary pattern these days. People move from one job to another and from one place to another. And with increasing frequency, people are moving from one career to another. Even a housewife's work doesn't remain the same.

Instead of retirement (and with it something that is best described as termination), surely more appropriate to our changing circumstances and relevant to today's needs is another *transition* in a series of transitions. Perhaps that's more nearly the pattern that our work-lives and careers, whatever they have been, ought to take—namely, a series of transitions from one work or career phase to another, each adapted to changing resources of energy and consistent with changing interests and changing life goals. We are finding, for example, that more and more persons are retiring from a job (because it's mandatory) and then getting another job—and then reporting they are busier, and happier, than ever before. A woman I know, ninety-one years of age and totally deaf, lives in a retirement residence. But if you should decide to drop in some morning to visit, you're likely not to find her in. Every day she leaves the residence to spend a good part of her day doing volunteer work as a visitor at a nursing home down the street. It fits her current interests and level of energy. And it gives her an important reason to get up in the morning.

It is interesting to note in this respect that according to Sula Benet, the anthropologist who lived for many months among the Abkhasians (the long-living people of the Russian Caucasus), these people have no word in their language for retirement. They live to be 110, 115, and older, and the expectation of the later years is positive and optimistic. For them, late life for the very old in no way disconnects from earlier life. Alexander Leaf of Harvard University, another student of the lives of these people at close hand, has come to the conclusion that such continuity of activity contributes greatly to their unusually long lives.

Beyond the idea of a continuing work-life, I must repeat, is the consideration that as people get on in years (and your oldster is one of them), they are indeed very likely to undergo a change in interests and a change in goals. There is nothing as drastic as a change in personality, but rather a shift in focus, a coming to value some things more while valuing other things less. It doesn't seem unreasonable that accumulated experience should lead to such an outcome.

There is no rule that says once a barber always a barber; once a teacher always a teacher; once a housewife, dentist, bus driver, clerk, attorney, secretary, mechanic, tailor, engineer, always that! People change in many ways as they grow older; not the least to be expected is change in interests, aspirations, hopes, and dreams.

Early preparation for the later years may be a fine notion for the future aged, but what about those in

their sixties or seventies or eighties right now who
have not prepared? You might be tempted ("for his
own good," of course!) to push, coerce, or manipu-
late that older person you care for into doing something he is not capable of doing or is steadfastly unwilling to do. By the same token, it is not at all helpful
to define that older person's work or social role in one
unvarying way, or to encourage him to do so. You
want to avoid, on your part, boxing that person in and
closing up potentialities and new capabilities yet to
be discovered, explored, and developed in that person.
What is worst of all, you want to avoid denying that
older person a fuller and more satisfying life in his
later years by cutting him off from the necessary
transitions from one activity (work) to another.

There are mature adults who like to say that their
work is their whole life (this is very often true of people in professions, including show business). They
appear to believe it and act upon it. But it's a rare
bird, indeed, who, given the proper encouragement
and inclination, does not sooner or later discover a
whole new set of interests within himself. Perhaps
with some digging your elder might uncover unsus-
pected, hidden talents. If you were to take the trouble
to review the life history and activities of your parent,
you would undoubtedly begin to uncover inner resources and potentials you hadn't guessed existed. Sit
down with your oldster. Talk it over. Explore! Don't
try to do it all at once. But ask some questions! Make
a list! Help him discover what he might not by himself. You can also help your oldsters relate what is discovered in this process to opportunities all around
them that put a premium on their rich fund of experience, wisdom, practical know-how, and dependa-

bility. Now, in their later years, it is precisely these qualities that have added value and should by all means be directed into useful functions.

Let's back up for a moment to the retired repair shop owner described earlier. Here, indeed, was a man who defined his whole life as his business, and vice versa—a truism that both he and his son seemed to accept without question. As a result both viewed him from a single perspective—a manager, the boss. Yet no doubt in these retirement years he could make extremely valuable contributions in different ways than being boss, which is what counseling eventually helped them discover. Dad, for example, could keep his eye on the books—after all, he was as dependable as daylight, knew the business well, and had kept the books for years. He could take on the important responsibility of scheduling repair jobs or overseeing final quality control in the shop. The trouble was that it had apparently not occurred to them to spell all this out and come to some agreement on it. The problems that grew out of the father's living with his daughter and son-in-law were even more difficult to deal with because of the daughter's guilty feeling about any suggestion regarding alternative living arrangements—and Dad's finesse at playing upon that guilt. Eventually she was able to come to terms with herself about that—and with Dad.

An attorney friend of mine retired from the practice of law in New York and subsequently moved to the West Coast with his wife. They were childless, had sufficient income to maintain themselves comfortably, and seemed in a good position to enjoy their "golden years." Yet he was strangely restless and uncertain. He knew what he *didn't* want. He didn't want any more of a sixty- or seventy-hour week; he knew he didn't want to practice law; he knew he didn't want to fish, travel, or play cards seven days a week.

In the course of our conversations, I discovered he had been known in his neighborhood back in New York as Mr. Fixit! He was very adept with his hands. The broken electric coffeepot, the burned-out toaster, the disabled bicycle—all these and more were brought to him by friends and neighbors. And with great patience, skill, and pleasure he fixed them. Yet, curiously, he had never made the connection in his mind between this skill, the delight he took in it, and the restlessness and disenchantment of his early retirement experience.

One can quite easily imagine this gentleman spreading the word around his neighborhood and community that he would take in small appliances and "fixit" repair jobs. What a relief for neighbors to know that, instead of taking their defunct electric pot downtown and leaving it there for two weeks for repairs that would likely cost about nine dollars (for a twenty-three dollar pot), they could take it to him, leave it for a couple of days, and get a good job done for five dollars. Thus, this man, in continuing to provide a useful and needed service in his neighborhood (for pay!) while doing something that fascinated and pleased him, made a nice "career" transition.

It is not only paper and tin cans that can be recycled! Please begin to appreciate what the notion of transition can mean, especially in the later years. The work-life need not be one narrow, monotonous track until retirement is reached and then a terminal state, leading into a sort of limbo until deterioration and death occur. People are far more important than paper and tin cans, but transitional phases in the later years that fit in with a senior's physical energy and capacity and changing life goals and interests are a kind of recycling in human terms. In the long run such transitions represent the brightest hopes for the future well-being of our aged. In the long run, too, it means the difference between health and illness, the difference between competence and incapacity.

It is important not to be put off by your awareness of disabilities in your elderly parent. Being a person with a disability is not the same as being a disabled person. That only describes a person with a certain constraint. An older individual with chronic diabetes or chronic arthritis or chronic bad eyes is not incurably sick. Given these constraints, that individual can be as healthy as anyone else. Health and disease (disability) *can* coexist in any individual; the disability may only mean shifting to another set of potentialities and capabilities. An individual with paralyzed legs who can learn to work with his hands (or eyes or mouth or ears) is no more disabled than the blind pianist-singer Ray Charles.

And when you encourage and help the older person to shift course and discover potentials, don't be too easily discouraged by a few false starts. It's not always easy to start on a new track, especially for those not especially adventuresome to begin with. Such discovery trips should begin with much encouragement and support and should be easy enough in the early stages to insure some feeling of accomplishment, some satisfaction, and some success.

Keep in mind, too, that there is always the possibility that every suggestion you make to your oldster might be countered with essentially the same response, "I'm not interested" or "I don't want to." Needless to say, any person who persists in responding to any and all suggestions with an unvarying "yes, but . . ." may either have an altogether different life agenda or be intent on diddling, annoying you, or getting back at you.

Some people have expressed the concern that "recycling" older persons into new careers may hurt the economy because that would keep others out of jobs. There is no reason to believe that our economy is designed like an enormous game of musical chairs, with so many chairs (jobs) to match so many players (workers). In order to provide seats for new players, according to such a notion, we must get rid of some of the old players. As a matter of fact, there are a great many kinds of services that our society truly needs and wants that perhaps only the elderly among us are willing and capable of providing. Take the Foster Grandparents Program, to name just one. How urgent and desperate is the need of a great many socially deprived youngsters! By definition, only an older person can be a foster grandparent and provide the care, attention, and affection the child needs. No teenager can adequately fill that role. What about peer counselors of older adults, to name another needed service. Or consumer protection monitors? Or trainers in certain crafts and skills? If you stopped to think about it, you could develop a substantial list.

The striking fact is that many older persons are already engaged in such useful and productive services. The only problem is how we choose to define productivity. We are far too used to doing things *for* our older citizens, so it is hard to see them as productive. When *they* engage in such services, society tends to define the activity in such a way as to minimize their productivity. Society customarily does that in a very subtle and clever way. For instance, in many if not most large and bureaucratic state or Veterans' Administration hospitals, a large number of the residents provide services (generally clerical or housekeeping) in varying degrees that help maintain the institution. These hospitals generally avoid paying these residents for their work (which is often the equivalent of that of the paid employees) by a very simple device— by calling the work they do "therapeutic." Naturally society doesn't pay people for their therapy, does it?

The same device is used in other areas dealing with older persons, especially if they are retired. They are labeled "volunteers," society reasoning that such activity is good for them, keeps them active, and so on. This may in itself be true but has little to do with the issue of monetary reward, which is important to all of us and at the same time symbolizes the merit and value of the service.

Imagine what would happen if on your next visit to your physician, for example, or your clergyman or attorney or teacher, you were to ask him if he likes his work. No doubt he'd tell you that he does. No doubt a major reason he's practicing medicine is to help people. But can you imagine the response you'd get if you were bold enough to say to him, "Why, that's fine. I'm glad you're in medicine to do good. That's why you really shouldn't charge me because what you're doing is also good for you! It keeps you active, involved, and in the mainstream." Isn't that often what we expect of our elderly who provide useful services?

Please do not misunderstand what I am saying. Volunteer work, especially if one can afford to do it, is great—at any age. One misses a splendid experience if one expects to be paid for every service rendered. Experience clearly demonstrates that volunteering for a common good is beneficial also for the spirit of the volunteer; it keeps one involved, busy, and in touch with the mainstream of life. There is even more to it. Volunteers are less likely to go on the public dole or to become overly dependent on public support, less likely to become cases that require special care. The payoff is, in general, a reduction of negative productivity and an increase in real contributions to the life of the neighborhood and community. As personal satisfactions of the elderly increase, so, too, does the social and economic stability of society in general. But at the same time I am arguing that this attitude toward volunteering ought not be used as a cover to hide a reluctance to reward an individual (also voluntarily) for his work where appropriate and necessary just because that individual happens to be old and retired.

Most elderly, if possible, should *not* retire. What we see modeled more and more today is the older person who retires from one job and begins working at another. This pattern has everything to recommend it if the work suits the individual's interests and capacities. You will do your elders a great service by giving them encouragement and support in their using themselves to the limits of their capacities and potentials.

Dostoevski made the point brilliantly: "If you wanted to punish a man so severely that even the most hardened criminal would quail, all you would have to do is make his work meaningless." We must help our elderly discover not punishment but promise in their later years.

5

Institutionalization— When, If Ever?

WHY THE FEAR OF INSTITUTIONS. . . .
INSTITUTIONALIZATION IS NOT RELATED TO GEOGRAPHY
—IT CAN OCCUR ANYWHERE. . . . WHAT A DIALOGUE
CAN DO FOR YOU. . . . MINICONTRACTS WITH AN AGING
PARENT. . . . WHEN YOU FEEL GUILTY. . . . HOW TO TELL
DEPENDENCE FROM OVERDEPENDENCE. . . . "PUTTING
YOUR PARENT AWAY" IS NO JOKE. . . . SURVIVAL AND
COMPETENCE. . . . THE INDIGNITY IN INFANTALIZING AN
AGING PARENT. . . . THE PLACE OF LEGITIMATE
SELF-INTEREST.

Even middle-agers who have a good, close relationship with aging parents may come to a point when they have to give some serious thought to the possibility of institutional living for their oldsters. This does not at all imply ill will or bad motives. Yet it must be admitted that this is a rather delicate subject. For many, it is an emotionally charged, sensitive issue. Even the thought of such a move makes some middle-agers feel guilty, as if they were being bad children.

We are going to consider this carefully. First, we need to take a candid look at what we mean by institutionalizing. Second, you need to consider when, if ever, you need to make living arrangements outside of the home for your elderly parent. Third, if you come to such a decision, how do you go about making

95

appropriate arrangements? Fourth, how do you select an alternative living situation?

All such considerations have to do with related questions like, Should an older parent be encouraged to live by himself? Should elderly parents live with their children, and do they prefer to do so? When and how is the decision made to have them move? How can you tell if an institution (a retirement residence or nursing home) is a good one or not? These are the questions we shall try to answer in this and the following chapter.

For openers, we might as well acknowledge that most people have the impression (when they think about it at all) that institutions are pretty bad places to live. To most people the word *institution* has the connotation of "the end of the line," "the bottom of the barrel," as far as decent living is concerned. No doubt that's because the very word *institution* stirs up a mental image of an unattractive, dismal-looking building; bland, unexciting, tasteless food; a monotonous, boring, routine way of life; lack of variety; lack of privacy; few if any opportunities to make decisions or have control over one's daily activities; and isolation of the individual from the mainstream of life in our society.

All of these circumstances are commonly (and correctly) believed to lead to apathy, overdependence, loss of initiative, depression, and loss of self-esteem on the part of the resident. At that point it is said that the worst has happened—the resident is said to be institutionalized. More often than not, that is the main reason many middle-aged sons and daughters put off a decision and struggle to keep their aging parent in their own home.

At one time I shared the belief that the very nature of institutional life, simply because it was institutional, would inevitably lead to the result just described. But I think that view no longer is reliable or necessarily accurate. It is not that institutions by nature are "bad." It is more fair and more accurate to point out that *bad* institutions are bad. "Good" institutions are something quite different. A good institution can be quite helpful and can serve a very useful purpose.

To this we must add the observation that institutionalization is not a matter of geography; that is, it is not related to location. Elderly people living in settings other than an institution can come to be just as institutionalized, with just as bad results as in a "bad" institution. Consider how easily this can happen. For example, an aging mother lives with her daughter and son-in-law and their family. Mother has her very own clean, nicely decorated room. But her middle-aged daughter continually exhorts Mother not to cook in the kitchen because she says, "You know, Mother, the kitchen gets all messy and dirty, and I haven't time to do the extra cleaning up." Daughter also reminds Mother, "You do forget to turn off the stove sometimes, Mother," and then adds, "I would rather you wouldn't cook for the family, Mother, because you don't cook what we like."

In addition, the daughter urges Mother to stay in her room on Saturday and Wednesday nights and watch TV because those are the evenings (Daughter says) "we'd like to have some friends in for company." Not only that, but Daughter urgently advises Mother over and over again not to go out on her own because Mother might "get hurt" or "get lost." At the same time Daughter tells her mother, "I'd love to take you here or there, Mother, but I do have my volunteer work to attend to and errands to run and the household shopping to do—I just don't have the time to be taking you around, much as I'd like to."

Obviously, one might elaborate on these kinds of instances that occur in a private home. From her point of view, this middle-aged daughter is not being unreasonable. We can thus envision just such a set of circumstances in which the elderly parent *not* living in an institution but rather in a private dwelling, because of many constraints and restrictions, could still become much more institutionalized than if living in a congregate (institutional) setting that provides all those things that make for a viable and worthwhile way of life: variety, adventure, interesting things to do, people to talk to and care about—and most important of all, a meaningful role in daily living. The paramount issue, then, is not so much the place where the older person might live as what the conditions and circumstances of daily living for the older person all add up to. Location is only one small consideration here. It would probably be more useful, then, when you do consider the possibilities, to do so in terms of alternative living arrangements rather than in terms of "putting them away" in an institution.

That seems to be a different and more useful frame of reference within which to determine when and what kind. Keep in mind that alternative living arrangements have become a new option for families in recent years. Circumstances of life *have* changed— and are changing—radically. The extended family, in which three and even four generations lived and worked together in pretty much a self-contained and self-sufficient family unit (often in a rural setting), has for the most part disappeared, perhaps forever. The sense of "place," of belonging, and of clearly defined roles and all the built-in supports that go along with that earlier way of life seems to be disappearing, too, in the process. This is especially so for aging parents.

Certainly there are many situations where older parents can and do enjoy a congenial relationship within the homes of middle-aged sons and daughters. But where it happens that the middle-agers are away from home most of the time pursuing their own careers, it may be impossible for them to create or arrange the kind of challenging, viable way of life for their elderly that we are talking about. This is not to imply that it is necessary for someone to be at home all the time. But if your oldster is unable to get around very well on his own—perhaps even needs some assistance to manage adequately and as a result is virtually isolated most of the time—then it's time to give serious consideration to an alternative form of living. There is no general rule to cover this. Every case is different and has to be considered on its own merits.

We certainly can cite many instances where an older person (especially a woman) is able to some extent to maintain some roles and some activities he or she had been accustomed to as a younger person. If both Mom and Dad are away from home earning money or pursuing careers, wouldn't it make considerable sense to encourage Grandma and Grandpa to use their experience and skill in helping with the preparation of food or cleaning or planning or doing the family accounts or some other useful family duties? This doesn't mean that Grandma or Grandpa ought to be taken merely as unpaid housemaids, maintenance men, or built-in children- or house-sitters. Older persons do have a right to exercise their own options and need encouragement to pursue their own goals, their own hobbies, their own work, and their own interests.

What this does mean is that you can and should conscientiously try to discover compatible roles for your oldster within the family setting. The degree of your success in doing so will in large measure depend upon the spirit of openness, imagination, compromise, acceptance, and goodwill that you bring to the task. Whether or not older parents should continue to live with their middle-aged children will also depend upon how emotionally and socially compatible all concerned find themselves to be. Face this issue realistically as well as sentimentally. If your repeated experience, including the help of understanding and sensitive professional counseling should you choose to get it, continues to demonstrate that the persons living under one roof annoy, irritate, or prove abrasive to each other because of conflicts in life-style or life goals, then obviously no useful purpose is going to be served in continuing to live together. An accumulation of unresolved conflicts can only lead to hidden resentments that only further alienate and penalize both the older parent and the middle-aged children. There is certainly no sense in blindly and stubbornly forcing the continuation of this kind of living arrangement.

Can any kind of satisfactory accommodation be worked out between middle-agers and their elderly parent where the relationship is not a particularly happy one, but where for a variety of reasons other living arrangements cannot easily be made? It is easy to imagine instances where you can honestly say you care for your elderly parent but find it terribly difficult to get along with that person in the same house. This is such a common human problem. Living together is best described as a continuous stream of interlocking, interacting events, conditions, and transactions. This flow of events across time consists of a series of arrangements people make with each other, spoken or unspoken, formal or informal. In effect, we may characterize these arrangements as a series of contracts that we make with each other. Marriage involves the very same sort of thing, and the same kind of arrangements are also worked out with young children. There is really no valid reason whatsoever why arrangements or minicontracts cannot be worked out with an elderly parent in the very same manner. It doesn't matter whether it's a formal agreement or an informal, simple, verbal arrangement (depending upon your style and preferences). You might find it fairly comfortable to begin with something like this: "We'd love to have you live with us, but let's talk about it and work out some agreements that will help give direction to all of us." In just such a simple way as that the middle-aged offspring can ask elderly parents about their willingness to undertake certain obligations or roles (or at least begin to explore and discuss these). In turn, the preferences and responsibilities of the younger adults in the house can be outlined and then gone over in sufficient detail so that everyone understands what's going on, and has a chance to talk about it. The goal, according to this notion, is to establish ground rules of participation through a pooling of resources and responsibilities that everyone can agree on. Perhaps an elderly father can help with gardening, minor maintenance, or with housekeeping. Grandma might be able to assist with food preparation, planning, or keeping track of the budget. This isn't meant to suggest what family members *should* do, but is an indication of one of many patterns of arrangements that can be made to fit any particular family's requirements.

It would be taking a long stride toward eliminating ambiguity or misunderstanding if elderly parents could get a good "reading" of what the limits are as well as the expectations. For their part, the middle-agers will know quite clearly what is expected of them. This kind of formula, if open to reconsideration and renegotiation at some later time, can be enormously helpful in preventing conflict and avoiding a lot of irritation between those generations living under one roof.

As far as alternative living arrangements are concerned, is there one most important factor to consider before making a decision? No one general answer will precisely fit every individual situation. There is no good substitute for a careful and thoughtful examination of your particular circumstance. Try to determine to what extent you are realistically able to provide a viable and congenial way of life for your parent. You have an obligation to try to determine what your oldster's interests, desires, and life-style preferences truly are. If all that is rationally and fairly explored to its full extent, the odds are that you will be able to determine together which step to take and when to take it, and what kind of alternative living arrangement to begin to look for.

The biggest obstacle in considering alternative living arrangements, to say nothing of actually proposing them, commonly seems to be the terrible feelings of guilt—"I'm putting my parent away." In order to get over guilt, it's very important to deal head on with your feeling of betrayal of the older person. The fact of the matter is that an alternative living arrangement may be the best service you could offer the parent under certain conditions. Let's just assume for the moment that you have come to the conclusion together that your elderly parents need the kind of attention, certain activities, and other services that they cannot get in full measure while living with you. Let's also assume it's possible for them to get what they want and need in some alternative living arrangement. What possible good, then, would be served in *not* making the move in such a circumstance? An alternative living arrangement in that case is *not* "putting them away." Such an arrangement, rather, turns out to be a very positive step in response to a clear and immediate need.

Old age in and of itself does not make an individual infirm or incompetent or unable to manage adequately. Several disabilities may already be present. And the manner in which any older person copes with the activities and requirements of daily living may not always be consistent with the expectations of middle-aged sons and daughters. But that is quite another issue and another problem. What is more important is that the middle-agers be extremely cautious in coming to conclusions about the ability of an older person to fend for and take care of himself and his own interests. For one thing, aging parents have already managed to survive a lengthy span of time, and no doubt in most instances with a fair degree of success. That surely says something about their capabilities—past, present, and potential. All right, where does that lead us? To the matter of dependence—and overdependence. We need to avoid slipping into an extreme position on either side because that's not desirable either. The problem was neatly characterized by a middle-aged daughter who put it this way:

> It's not that I don't care for or am not concerned about my elderly parents. But I do want to live my life and don't want, in a sense, to have to carry them around on my back.

Most older persons, when asked, will immediately insist that they don't want to encumber their children. In most instances these same elderly parents are extremely reluctant to live with their middle-aged children, primarily (they say) because they are so fearful of becoming a burden.

Because the multiple losses that begin to accumulate in the later years so easily lend themselves to greater opportunities for dependence, we need to be very precise about the meaning of "dependent" and "independent." I don't think it's so controversial to insist that it's only the rare individual who is completely independent. By far, most of the rest of us are very dependent, relatively. We are dependent upon each other for a great many things (with few true pioneer types left). Therefore, being dependent in and of itself is not so bad. Family members are dependent upon each other for love, affection, nurturance, support, loyalty, and a lot more. We, in society, depend upon each other, especially in urban areas, for many goods, services, and much more. It's not dependency that causes problems in a family; rather it's the degree of dependency with which we're concerned.

In most instances, with the passage of years comes the need for somewhat greater dependence, for a variety of reasons in a variety of circumstances. Dad, for example, who was always a very independent fellow, may begin in his later years to do something he has never done before. He may begin to consult with his middle-aged son about saving money and making investments, ask his opinion and seek his advice. He may ask his son to help with some of his banking transactions. He may ask for assistance with transportation. There are many possibilities. This may flow in part from less energy on Dad's part, from a sense that his son is more in touch or up-to-date with information, perhaps from awareness of his own memory lapses, or maybe even from a bit of distrust of his own judgment in certain matters. Or it might be for any number of personal reasons. Such requests, as indications of some increased dependency, may tempt the middle-aged son to become annoyed with Dad's overdependence or to conclude that Dad is slipping. The son might thus easily be seduced into literally taking over Dad's affairs, which may seem offhand to be the simplest solution. Since he asked, no doubt Dad needs *some* assistance. The question is how much assistance, and the danger is to assume too much.

A case in point was reported to me by a social worker who interviewed an elderly woman living alone in her large home in a Los Angeles suburb. The woman was a widow. Her children were long since grown up, married, and with families of their own. She preferred to stay in the rambling old house where she had spent most of her married life and raised her children. This arrangement, however, was of great concern to her children. They kept arguing with her how risky it was for her to live by herself. They would repeatedly remind her of all the terrible things that could happen to her there in her solitary way of life. Their main worry was that she might fall one day and lie helpless for hours. Out of their great concern they kept urging her to move into a retirement residence or some other kind of congregate living. But she would have none of this. She preferred to stay in her comfortable, familiar surroundings, which she dearly loved. She admittedly didn't keep up her home as well as she once did, but she simply couldn't bring herself to leave the scene of a thousand treasured memories and associations.

Each of the children would call their mother almost daily. And almost daily, each child would caution the mother not to walk down the basement stairs and not to walk up the attic stairs. And because this was driving that dear old lady up the wall, she literally pleaded with the social worker (who had arranged a visit at the children's request):

> The best thing you can do for me is to get my children to leave me alone. I am glad they are concerned about me. I know that there are risks in my living by myself, but I'm willing to take the risks. I am their mother, not their child. Please tell them to treat me accordingly.

This droll but insightful incident tells us again about the importance of maintaining one's sense of self-esteem and self-respect through, for example, independence. How important it is for the aging parent— as it is for the middle-aged child! We simply have to become very sensitive to this need so that we can learn to recognize, each time, that very real but thin line separating true helpfulness from the takeover. Doing things for oneself is an important way to maintain a sense of effectiveness and competence. Doing something effectively or at least satisfactorily is the bedrock for feeling worthwhile, and it is a most necessary ingredient of positive self-regard. Taking over for an older person tasks that he can very well do for himself—even if not as quickly, efficiently, or stylishly as you could—is to infantalize the older person. That's not a service; that's demeaning and belittling.

A dramatic example of this problem of infantalizing the old is something I have observed on more than a few occasions in certain nursing homes I have visited—especially at mealtime. Get a picture in your mind's eye of three or four elderly residents seated in their chairs arranged in a semicircle around an aide and a table. There's a bowl of soup in front of each of these elderly residents. The aide is feeding each resident in turn from his own bowl, spooning soup into each mouth. These residents are called (in the technical jargon) "feeders."

Appalled when I first observed this, I asked how the situation came to be. There are a number of contributing factors, but one version given is as follows: Grandpa, who is a resident here (many such facilities seem to insist on referring to elderly residents as "patients"), was eating lunch one day when his daughter came to visit. It so happens that Grandpa has a pronounced shaking in his eating arm and when his daughter dropped in, she was just in time to observe him spilling a goodly amount of his lunch on his shirtfront and pants. Terribly distressed by the sight, she bolted out of the room and down the corridor, greatly agitated. She accosted the first staff person she laid eyes on and in a loud and angry voice demanded to know just what the place was being paid for, why Grandpa wasn't being helped, and so on.

You can believe, then, that these feeders as often as not are taking their food in this infantile manner so as to satisfy some relative and keep peace for the staff. Actually the problem—even the issue—is not simply some spilled food or a soiled shirt. After all, a paper napkin tucked under the chin would take care of that. The more basic and important issue is whether or not a soiled blouse or shirt is too high a price to pay for encouraging the older person to do something for himself in order to maintain some sense of competence and effectiveness. Older persons, even in institutions, do not need to be constantly attended to, dressed, spoon-fed, patted, wiped, and carried about (except in very rare instances) as if they were somewhat incompetent and inept children. They may, indeed, need certain kinds of assistance in certain situations. But to be treated like a baby or an awkward child does nothing to boost the morale or hoist the sagging spirit of a person who has already experienced multiple losses and the increasing sense of vulnerability that goes along with them.

So before you leap to the conclusion that your oldster can't take care of himself, whether in your home or his, you should conscientiously and realistically examine the situation. You will need to balance the fact that there are some things he or she doubtless cannot do as well as before, nor as quickly as before, with whatever can be discovered about his or her present inclinations, preferences, interests, incentives, and potentials. What needs to be avoided like the plague is the taking over of functions that the older person can in fact continue to perform. It's imperative to avoid imposing services and attention, whether professional or not, that are neither desired nor required.

The assumption under which middle-agers (or the professionals whose services they've sought) take over is that such assistance is not only necessary but welcomed. But that may not follow at all! There are always those elderly individuals who will not resist the unwelcome helping hand or even fight back at indignities. In some instances, this may happen because that particular older person is (and probably always was) a very passive individual. In other instances, it may be simply too difficult to mobilize the energy required to fight back; thus, the older person complies. Some who are stronger and more assertive by nature and training will resist. When they do, they may, therefore, be showing you more than mere crankiness, stubbornness, or rigidity. They may be showing you guts, an independent spirit, and courage, plus a strong need to feel competent. Others, much less strong and more passive, may fool you into thinking you're doing the right thing for them because they don't argue or resist, but go quietly along.

The decision about whether or not to look for a nursing home or alternative living arrangement seems to depend rather heavily on the middle-ager rather than on the elderly relative. Therefore, you need to appreciate the importance of carefully examining and weighing your own attitudes and the factors that affect you and your life. By the same token, please do appreciate the importance of developing an honest dialogue with that older person you care about. If you do that, it's safe to predict that in most instances you will get much important information from him or her, and you will learn a lot.

This means that you will need to work as much as possible toward a consensus between you and your aging parent. As early as possible, you and your parent should desensitize yourselves so that living arrangements, as an example, can be discussed openly, candidly, without anger and rancor, and without muddling the issue. When the day comes, if it ever does, when it looks as if alternative living arrangements are not only desirable but even necessary, it won't come upon any of you as an agonizing surprise or a day of trauma and pain. Rather it will come as a day that was anticipated and prepared for.

Admittedly, this is not always as easy to accomplish as it is to describe. But then we're not discussing baking cookies, for which there are recipes. We're talking about human relationships, for which there are no foolproof recipes. For instance, there are aged parents who, when dealing with their middle-aged children, are not above using the ploy of pressing certain kinds of sensitive, emotional "hot buttons." There are some older persons who have strong prejudices and even stronger negative feelings (at least at first) about alternative living arrangements. They do tend initially to feel they are being put away or being gotten rid of. They do respond to any such suggestion by trying to evoke guilt feelings in their children. You've probably heard this comment: "All right, if you want to put me away, go ahead . . . after all I've done for you. . . . That's the thanks I get for all the sacrifices I've made for you." Don't be put off by such dialogue. If you encourage a fair and open discussion about possible options and arrangements and advantages and disadvantages, and if you explore and investigate different types of accommodations over a period of time, then when a moment of decision does finally come, your aging parent is less likely to view the prospect as threatening or overwhelming. That sensitive, vulnerable person has had plenty of time to turn it over in his or her mind, to consider it calmly rather than under stress in a period of crisis. In that context your elder may see the issue, not as being "dumped" or put away, but as the most acceptable, creative solution to a common problem—yours and his.

Of course, there are older persons who, like others at an earlier age, are so conditioned that they simply will not listen to alternatives, much less discuss them. They simply make themselves inaccessible or unapproachable when the subject is broached. In such instances, when it appears to come down to a choice between agreement or sacrificing your life on the altar of another's whims or stubbornness, my own judgment is that there is a place for legitimate self-interest. We do this (insist upon our own rights) with our demanding youngsters, so why not with our demanding oldsters? You may in such a case have to take a deep breath and make up your mind to be gentle but unyieldingly firm. It is the same with anyone else in your life who proves unwilling to negotiate and compromise on something of such importance. You may have to say to Mom, "Our living arrangements here are really not as suitable as they might be. Rather than be in constant conflict with each other and suffer constant aggravation, we must talk together about alternatives that will make life better—more comfortable for you and for us. But I shall have to consider these alternatives, if I must, without your help." That is the time to be reasonably candid and as straightforward as you can, while avoiding being brutal or nasty. All you can do is put the need as kindly but as clearly and firmly as you can. And all the while, you can remind yourself that if you were to simply let it slide, out of a mistaken notion of kindness or peace at any price, you would likely be planting seeds that would grow and eventually bear the bitter fruit of resentment, perhaps even of anger and bitterness. The fact that you *do* care requires, in the end, that you be true to yourself and to your elderly.

6

Alternative Living—Selecting a Long-Term Care Facility

ENVIRONMENTS HAVE PERSONALITIES. . . . CONGREGATE
LIVING FOR ELDERLY. . . . RETIREMENT RESIDENCES. . . .
INTERMEDIATE CARE. . . . NURSING FACILITIES. . . . BOARD
AND CARE HOMES. . . . DO YOU CHECK THE COOK OR TASTE
THE FOOD? . . . THE COMMONEST COMPLAINT OF
NURSING-HOME RESIDENTS. . . . WHEN IS A HOME NOT A
HOSPITAL? . . . TESTING WITH YOUR NOSE. . . . LANDMARKS
AND STREET SIGNS. . . . FINDING OUT WHAT THE FACILITY
CAN DO AND CAN'T DO. . . . ALL PLAY AND NO WORK. . . .
IS THERE AN IDEAL FACILITY?

The places where people live, their environments, can be said to have personalities in some ways like human personalities. We all no doubt have met some people whom we would call warm, friendly, supporting. You really feel good being with such folks. Some environments are like that too. You enjoy being there.

On the other hand, some people are cold, even distant. They are polite enough, but you never feel quite comfortable with them. Some environments are like that. You never feel quite at home there. Some people are inviting. They make you feel welcome. So are some environments. Some people are extremely demanding. They seem able to put your teeth on edge and drain the energy out of you. Well, so are some environments.

I'm sure you can easily picture for yourself homes you've been in at some time or other, environments you've experienced that have had just such positive or negative effects on you. Sometimes, just as with our impressions of people, our first impressions of environments may be the correct ones. But in some instances, when we become more familiar with the environments, our impressions may change.

Perhaps that's one reason why many people believe institutions, particularly nursing homes (or retirement homes), are bad. Having gotten the impression that long-term care facilities for the aged isolate and dehumanize the resident, you and your aging parent may have little taste for such environments. And you may very well wonder where you might even begin in order to select one that will suit. There is really only one sure way to find out. It surely helps to get clues from friends who recommend one facility or another, but you and your aging parent have to investigate on your own. No one can do that for you.

As things now stand, you do have some range of choices with regard to the alternative living arrangements for your aging parent now available. In most locales you are likely to find four different kinds of long-term care available for your aging parent.

1. One is what is customarily referred to as a retirement residence or retirement home. Essentially this is very similar to apartment living. The residents of retirement homes are pretty much independent and self-sufficient; that is, they are required to be able to take care of themselves and to arrange for any special services they may need (including medical, dental, podiatric, and similar ones). Usually in retirement residences elderly persons do their own light house-

keeping and cook their own meals. In an increasing number of instances, however, a central kitchen and dining room are available, and sometimes housekeeping services are available too.

Formerly, retirement residences offered a life contract payment package. That meant that when an elderly person moved in, he turned over all his financial assets to the retirement home in exchange for which the home contracted to take care of that individual (room, board, and all services) for the rest of the resident's life. Increasing costs and inflation now prohibit that kind of arrangement. Practically all retirement residences have eliminated that kind of contract. Those that have not go bankrupt.

The typical financial arrangement today is the payment of what most call an accommodation fee. This can vary from as little as eight or ten thousand dollars to as much as twenty thousand or more, depending upon the type of accommodations and location. In addition to this, a monthly fee (for food and maintenance) is charged. This, too, varies from approximately three hundred dollars per month on up, depending upon the kind of accommodation, how large and how plush, where located, and what kinds of extras are provided.

2. A second category of alternative living arrangements is what is generally referred to as an intermediate-care facility (ICF). It may not be identified in just this way in all areas. The ICF is a technical designation for facilities that are licensed to provide *some* additional supportive services to elderly persons who require them because of certain disabilities. ICFs provide a staff that does housekeeping chores, helps with shopping, prepares and serves meals, and provides

some social and activities programs. Usually these facilities limit themselves to the elderly who are for the most part able to take care of themselves even though getting about may require the use of a walker or a cane. Sometimes an accommodation fee is charged in such facilities. More typically, a flat fee is charged for room and board, ranging, again, from about $350 per month on up. Many facilities will charge for extras, like laundry.

3. The third general category of living arrangements is the so-called nursing home. The most widely used technical designation for these facilities is "skilled nursing facility" (SNF). It's easy to be confused about this because a wide variety of names are commonly used: convalescent hospital, sanitarium, rest home, extended care facility. Some names are rather exotic and a few show delightful stretches of imagination: Garden of Eden Convalescent Hospital, Golden Age Rest Home, and so on. The name of the facility, to be sure, does not set the standard. What counts is that nursing homes in all states are licensed and highly regulated by statutes and regulations. Usually these facilities are regulated and periodically inspected (inspections are called surveys in some areas) by the respective local or state department of health.

Retirement residences are usually not licensed. But SNFs are. Requirements include a certain number of staff for a given number of residents; a certain number of registered nurses (at least one for every ninety-nine residents); regular visits by physicians; and services by pharmacists, podiatrists, occupational and physical therapists, and activities directors. There is a procession through the SNF that may include clergymen, dentists, social workers, psychologists, speech therapists, education specialists, and the like. How much consulting such professionals do largely depends upon the financial resources of the facility and the philosophy of the owner or administrator.

Regulations for nursing homes (SNFs)include minimum requirements for entry-level personnel and continuing education for staff, and requirements pertaining to health, safety, and, at least nominally, to quality of care. Indeed, the law mandates a host of do's and don'ts regarding daily operations and procedures, ranging from the allowable temperature in the hot-water pipes all the way through to the amount of salt in the hamburger and what kinds of containers milk can be stored in. The continuing licensure of nursing homes depends upon continued compliance with this complex array of regulations.

In addition to the licensing of the facilities themselves, the nursing-home administrator (not necessarily the owner; the SNF may be part of a chain) must also be personally and separately licensed. Licensing of administrators and facilities as we know it is of fairly recent vintage, dating back only to the late sixties. In recent years the licensing of SNF administrators has become increasingly formal and stringent. Each aspiring administrator must take and pass a lengthy written examination covering all aspects of state and federal regulations. Eligibility to take the exam now includes a certain level of experience (on-the-job training) in this field as well as academic achievement, although about a dozen states have either minimal or no requirements.

All except nine states also require each licensed administrator to take approved continuing education (CE) courses in order to renew the license. In thirty-three states licenses are renewable every two years. The continuing education requirements range from a low of ten hours per year (West Virginia) to a high of fifty hours per year (Kansas, New York, South Dakota). All states together list some 14,500 licensed nursing homes (SNFs).

4. To complete the picture, it might be added that a substantial number of elderly people live in board and care establishments. These are unlicensed; they are essentially boardinghouses that usually provide for anywhere from three to a dozen or so persons and are generally run by a woman who has converted an older, large dwelling into single "apartments." Usually no services are provided other than meals and perhaps some housecleaning.

All of this is simply intended to give you a general idea of what to expect and some hint of what governmental expectations are regarding long-term care. But what does it all mean—the licensing, the regulations, the educational requirements, the inspections? How does that help you select the right place? In the last analysis, such information will help you very little in making a choice—that is, unless all you are looking for is little more than a clean room and bed, food, medications, and limited physical care.

That's something, to be sure. But is it enough for your aging parent? Knowing something about the "pedigree" of a nursing home and the credentials of the administrator and staff tells you little if anything about the style, the tone, the atmosphere—in a word, the quality of life for the aged resident. It's as if you were to judge a restaurant not by how the food is served and how it tastes but rather by where the chef went to school, what kinds of stoves and cooking utensils it uses, its decor, and how extensive the menu is. Obviously, that's not where the payoff is.

If you visit and become acquainted with a number of nursing homes in your vicinity, one major impression you're likely to get is how styles vary from one facility to another. I believe you will also get a sense of the differences in the atmosphere, the climate, of the various facilities. Most of all, you are bound to notice how commonly, almost universally, nursing homes reflect and even imitate the atmosphere of the acute-care general hospital.

In physical appearance alone most nursing homes remind you of hospitals. The rooms (often miniwards) are usually off long corridors. The staff are often dressed in white uniforms. The nurses' stations are very prominent; often they are the first thing you see when you walk in. Even the language used apes the hospital. It's often embedded in the name of the place. You hear people speak of the number of beds (as if that were the center of life there), and those who live there are invariably labeled "patients."

Is that what you are looking for? Would you want your aging parent labeled and treated as a patient until he or she dies? Indeed, you might even ask yourself if your aging parent is sick. Many, if not most older people, have accumulated some rather permanent disabilities: chronic arthritis, chronic diabetes, poor hearing, lessened energy, and the like. In most instances these conditions do not respond to conventional treatment and cure, which is what is supposed to happen in an acute-care hospital.

Practically everyone knowledgeable about the aged today agrees that the commonest complaint of residents in a long-term care facility is loneliness. And loneliness is only slightly ahead of boredom, the intense need for affection, and the need for something worthwhile to do with oneself. If that is what the need is in these places, we must ask, How do medications cure loneliness? How do clean beds, clean floors, and clean kitchens help fight boredom? How do physicians' visits and registered nurses on duty attend to the need for affection?

In looking for the right place, the first question you should ask is, What about this place will help make life worthwhile for my aging parent? The hospitallike atmosphere and the emphasis on cleanliness and physical care and illness should not distract you from looking for answers to that basic question. General medical and surgical hospitals (acute-care hospitals), after all, are not designed or intended to provide a normal way of life. No one seriously disputes that. Acute-care hospitals are designed to provide some kind of treatment and cure, either through medicine, surgical procedures, or some other kind of technological intervention. The aim is to help the patient get better or get well and out of there as quickly as possible.

Long-term care (and this includes the so-called nursing homes), on the other hand, is an altogether different kind of enterprise. This is a place that, for the most part, is intended for permanent or relatively permanent living. Statistics show that many older persons who enter a long-term care facility finish their days there. But that doesn't, and shouldn't, mean that older persons and their families should view such facilities as places where people waste their time until death. Nor should they be operated with such a notion in mind, even though it appears in some instances as if that were the case.

The vast majority of aged parents who live in long-term care facilities do have chronic disabilities. The vast majority require, at most, perhaps one, two, or three hours of physical care a day. A relatively small number of residents are totally bedfast. Is it certain that that's the way the bedfast must be? Many competent professionals seriously dispute it. Some aging parents (and yours may be one) appear to be confused, disoriented, forgetful, and given to wandering. Yet these are things about which something can be done. And that will be detailed in a little bit. But it's what you ought to look for and ask about.

Keep in mind that there is something even worse—much worse—than a facility with not-too-clean floors or so-so food or a facility that doesn't boast a plush dayroom or an all-stainless-steel kitchen. I am not making a case against good food or clean floors. What I am reminding you is that there is something more important to look for. You will want to look for a facility that does not virtually ignore or neglect those things that make life truly worthwhile for your aging parent. That would be the ultimate irony: having to live out his or her life in a neat, clean, orderly, well-run, sterile warehouse.

As you go about the business of choosing a place, you must ask yourself, "What will my aging parent's 'career' be like in this setting? Will it be enough to spend most of his (or her) day staring at the floor—even if it's a spotlessly clean floor?" It's easy to see that under certain conditions emotional, social, or psychological death may occur long before your aging parent's physical demise. I think that more often than we suspect, the death of an older parent has been hastened because he or she came to believe there was nothing more to live for. There was no longer any good reason to get up in the morning, which is the necessary ingredient in making any life worthwhile.

The basic task in selecting a long-term care facility, then, is to try to discover a facility that does not inadvertently hasten the end, but rather does everything it can to make life worth living. Given this frame of reference, you are already in a position to ask the right questions and to look for the things that truly matter. More specifically, where do you begin?

Begin at the point where you would start in looking for a house to buy or an apartment to rent. Start with location if the area is important to you and your aging parent. The neighborhood may seem unimportant if you assume your parent will spend all his time within the confines of the institution. But that assumption may mislead you. The occasion may arise when your parent will want to get out for a walk (or a wheelchair ride), purchase something at a store, window-shop, or whatever. The surrounding neighborhood should be the kind of environment that will encourage such activity. Neighborhoods that are high-crime areas or full of constant and dense traffic can be very forbidding to elderly persons and make them virtual prisoners in their own dwellings.

A person who wants and needs to continue getting around obviously requires a facility where shops, businesses of various types, and perhaps even a shopping center with a variety of stores are readily accessible. If such stores are located miles from the home or there are physical barriers such as having to go up a long hill to get to them, that's surely enough to discourage all but the most enterprising. Don't be surprised if, under such circumstances, the individual spends much of his or her life within the institutions.

Even if your parent isn't prepared to visit the surrounding neighborhood now, don't foreclose on future possibilities. That means it may be wise to visit the area more than once if everything else looks good. You'll want to visit it in the evening (is there undue noise at night?) or on a weekend. Some neighborhoods that have a lot of traffic during some portion of the day may be quite free of it at other times.

When you walk into the facility, make good use of all your senses. Use your nose; the sense of smell gives a great deal of information. If there are extremely disagreeable odors (for example, a strong smell of urine), walk around and try to discover if this has resulted from a minor accident or if this is a sign of very sloppy housekeeping. You might check that out again on your second or third visit. An occasional accident will always happen. But if bad odors are constant and pervasive, that's quite a different matter.

I would keep my eyes open to see if the place is reasonably clean and well kept or if it has the grubby, dingy look that suggests continuous neglect. Remember, an occasional lack of tidiness may merely be a sign of a place well lived in. That's not bad. Also, I would pay attention to other kinds of odors. Does it have a hospitallike antiseptic smell? Can you at mealtime smell the aromas of good home cooking that stimulate the residents to eat? Or does the whole place, even at mealtime, reek of Pine Sol?

Is the facility inside well lighted and well marked so it's easy to find your way around, easy to know where things and places are located? If you find it difficult to get around or if you get lost, why should you suppose it would be easier for your aging parent?

Are there plenty of landmarks, cues, and signs inside, and are they easy to use? Can you imagine what it would be like if you had to drive freeways or streets without signs, landmarks, or other cues? Pay considerable attention to that because—especially for an older person who may sometimes forget or who may simply find it difficult to get accustomed to a new environment—those signs and landmarks are tremendously important sources of orientation.

Not only should there be signs and other guideposts present, but these should be large enough and have numerals or letters clear enough for easy identification. What about clocks? Are they located so they can be clearly and easily seen by someone with faulty vision, or are they hidden in some nook or corner and too small to be easily read? Are there legible calendars around so residents can easily keep in touch with the day and date? Pay close attention to these and other devices that make it easy to find one's way around and through the environment, for such cues can make the difference between a facility in which people with disabilities can function competently and a facility where they are so penalized that they cannot cope very well at all.

An example of that which is decorative and attractive but which actually penalizes many older persons is the overstuffed sofa, the deep-sit couch. Such couches may look terribly comfortable, but have you ever observed an elderly person whose joints are stiff with arthritis sink into one of these pieces of furniture and then try to get up again—without help?

By the same token, what about regular chairs that have no arms, that is, which provide no support for getting up and sitting down? Speaking of chairs, consider the disadvantages of facilities with fifty- to sixty-foot-long corridors devoid of chairs where a person could sit and rest for a moment. To an older person who needs to conserve energy, trying to negotiate a long corridor with no convenient place to stop and rest can be an unnecessary strain.

Physical layout and well-planned interiors can play an enormous role in helping your parent feel secure and at home. Does the place encourage people to socialize by making it easy to do so? Does it allow enough privacy to make possible the developing and maintaining of a relationship of confidant? Having a confidant is crucial in weathering life's crises.

What about the color of the walls? Are they bright and intense enough to stimulate someone with poor vision? Is there reading material that has large print available and enough bright light to make reading a delight and not a discouraging chore? Perhaps you would want to ask about the availability of "talking" books or volunteers who can read to a person who is blind or whose sight is much diminished. These things are just a tiny sample of the many kinds of things that contribute to the worthwhileness of life because they all help to compensate in one way or another for losses and disabilities.

Isn't the attitude of the staff an important consideration? Emphatically yes! I would strongly urge you to spend time observing the residents and how they seem to be getting along—how the employees relate to the residents and how they treat them. Not only are the obvious gestures important, but equally so are some less obvious ones. It is not simply a matter of whether a staff person says good morning in a pleasant tone of voice. More important is whether the employee responds to the older person as a sensible human being or treats him or her in a patronizing way, as if dealing with a not-too-bright child.

Most older people, for obvious reasons, become enormously sensitive to these kinds of responses and gestures. There is a very great difference between feeling one is being taken seriously as a human being and being treated with dignity and feeling one is being treated in a casual, demeaning manner. Remember, your parent's self-esteem is at stake. It's important to try to observe if the employees seem to understand how intense and unremitting is the need for affection, warmth, and understanding.

Also, spend time talking with the administrator and some assistants. Try to discover their attitudes about making life worthwhile for those in their care. Certainly you should not hesitate to make it clear to them your expectations of the institution in which the elderly person you care about will be living. It's fair to ask for a clear statement of what the facility can do and what it cannot reasonably do. For instance, you might be inclined to ask if they will provide supervision for your aging parent. And the administrator may answer, "Yes!" But what does that really mean? Twenty-four-hour eyeball-to-eyeball supervision? It's doubtful if any facility would provide that, even if anyone seriously wanted it.

I had the opportunity to visit a nursing home that enjoyed a fairly good reputation for providing reasonably decent care. When it came to cleanliness, one could find no fault. The floors were spotlessly clean; the windows sparkled; the beds and linens were scrupulously crisp and clean. The kitchen, too, was spotless, and there was considerable evidence that the home provided reasonably good and tasty food. A physician visited regularly, ample medications were available, and a nurse, as well as other required staff, was on duty twenty-four hours a day.

The end of my tour brought me into a rather large dayroom. It was very attractive and bright, thanks to a large skylight. Yet I was appalled to see in this large room about thirty-five wheelchairs, and some benches, positioned around the perimeter of the room, in which the elderly people were sitting. Most of the people seemed to be either staring off vacantly into space or slumped over, sound asleep. Everywhere I walked in this facility, it was almost deathly quiet.

What can you say about a place like that? If physical care is all you're looking for, you cannot fault it. Yet, I believe places like that can turn out to be enormously destructive of the human spirit. The lack of variety, stimulation, and all the other vital features I have discussed is glaringly evident in such a supervisory atmosphere. It is almost a sure bet that you are going to see increasing signs of what appears to be senility among the residents; that is, there is going to be more forgetting, confusion, disorientation, apathy, and all the bad things we think of when we think about institutionalization in spite of the fact that the facility is clean and orderly. The horror of such a facility is that it turns out to be a well-run, orderly warehouse, and that is a factor you need to keep clearly in mind when you come to making judgments about and selecting a facility.

The most desirable facility will literally saturate its week with a wide variety of activities to suit a wide variety of tastes and needs. It will offer a veritable smorgasbord of opportunities for different residents to engage themselves in interesting and useful endeavors. These activities need not and should not be merely play. That's not what worthwhile living is all about, even for people with some disabilities or some diminished capacities. There needs to be opportunity for recreation and entertainment, of course. Variety and adventure, after all, are the spice of life and an effective antidote to boredom. But so are work and service. These provide the opportunity to feel needed and useful. It's important to continue to feel that you still count for something—at seventy and eighty and ninety and beyond.

You'll not only look for such opportunities for your aging parent in considering a facility, but will also weigh how appropriate the opportunities really are. In other words, you're not going to simply ask for a list of activities. Here's an example of what I mean.

I remember very well one elderly woman I met one day in a nursing home. With her shock of silvery hair she was very distinguished-looking, even though she was quite thin, almost emaciated. As I walked through the ward, she called me over to speak to her. She explained how she had been a practicing physician in southern California for almost forty-five years. As she spoke, I could tell she was a very bright, articulate, and well-educated woman. She had lost most of her family except for some relatives on the East Coast with whom she was not in touch. Eventually the time came when she could no longer support a home to live in and decided she had to have some other place to live. So at eighty-two years of age she moved into the particular facility I was visiting.

About the second week she was there, to her great embarrassment, she suffered a little accident, a matter of incontinence. An aide she had summoned was very responsive and took the woman's hospital gown away to have it changed. Unfortunately, the aide was not sensitive to the effect of walking away with the soiled gown leaving this lady naked, sitting on her bed, waiting for the next hour and a half for the aide to return with a clean gown. All the woman could do was to try to cover herself with a sheet.

This, however, was not the final indignity experienced by this proud and sensitive woman. What really disturbed and offended her, she explained, was that two weeks following that incident she had been invited to the activities room. She accepted the invitation because she felt she wanted to be doing something. When she got there, to her absolute chagrin, she discovered that the residents were cutting egg cartons lengthwise, coloring them, putting them in a circle around a base, stringing them together with yarn, and thus making wastebaskets.

Any one of us can surely imagine what it must have been like for that woman, a highly trained professional, articulate and skilled, to be "challenged" in such a demeaning and belittling way. This is a bit of what I mean when I refer to the need for activities to be appropriate and suitable to the individual's interests, preferences, life-style, and level of skills. I cannot put it too strongly that the activities should be of such a nature and of such quantity and variety that they do, in fact, provide as many options and opportunities as possible for the older person to maintain a real interest and a sense of adventure and variety in his or her daily life.

On another occasion, I was talking to a group of staff people at a long-term care facility about these issues. I recall vividly how the director of nursing, with great delight in her voice, enthusiastically explained how a few months before they had taken a group of residents to the local zoo for a day's outing. She described how excited they were and how almost like children in their enthusiastic response to the experience. I asked this trained professional if she recalled the last time the facility had arranged anything like this. Her response—stated seriously—was that a similar excursion to the zoo had taken place about eight months earlier. Wouldn't you agree that if the only chance you and I had for some adventure to fight boredom was on a twice-a-year basis, we would most likely go out of our minds? Wouldn't we begin to act in a senile way?

The majority of facilities provide at least the minimum with respect to physical care and health. They still have a long way to go. Some are so bad they should really be put out of business—the sooner the better. These include the out-and-out rip-off as well as those facilities that still seem to view their business as warehousing of the old. But for most, that "long way to go" simply means they need to learn to use more effectively the means at hand to provide a more viable way of life for their elderly residents. There are encouraging signs that more and more facilities are beginning to move in the right direction. They need all the public support and encouragement they can get. And facilities do exist—though not nearly enough as yet—that by dedicated, imaginative, and humane management do provide opportunity for a worthwhile way of life that should warm our hearts. That's what you should look for.

There is no more the perfect or ideal facility than there is the perfect or ideal home, human nature being what it is. The trick of the game is to try to find that kind of facility that *most nearly* matches the kind of ideal that we have in our minds. To that end I think we can all help in a sympathetic and collaborative way by associating ourselves with the people who run such facilities. We can encourage them to get an even larger vision of what their enterprise is all about and can assist to provide the input and stimulation and all the rest that it takes to make life more worthwhile for people living in a long-term care facility. Your help, if offered in the right way, will be appreciated. And it will make a big difference.

A concluding point needs to be emphasized. From a legal and moral standpoint, an elderly parent who has chosen one such alternative living arrangement should feel he or she has the freedom to move if the situation turns out to be not at all satisfactory. You do, indeed, have the option of finding another place that is much more congenial and suitable. Often people get the idea that once you help your parent move into a facility, you are really stuck and for legal reasons can't make a change. Or sometimes people get the notion that every other facility may be just as uncongenial or just as unsuitable. That's simply not so! Different facilities offer a variety of options, opportunities, and life-styles.

Having conscientiously investigated what is available to you, and having explored the alternatives with the older person you care for and care about through discussion and visits, you should be able to make a sensible and suitable choice. You can rest secure in the conviction that you have done the best you can to serve both your own best interests and those of your aged parent. In that spirit you can keep the supportive, affectional bonds between you strong and enduring right up to the end.

7

Death and Dying— How Do You Handle It?

DEATH, THE LAST GREAT EXPERIENCE OF LIFE. . . . FACING
OUR OWN MORTALITY. . . . FEELINGS ABOUT DYING
AND DEATH—HOW TO COME TO TERMS. . . . GRIEVING,
A NATURAL PROCESS. . . . SHARED GRIEVING. . . . SIGNS
AND SIGNALS OF REACTION TO BEREAVEMENT. . . .
DEATH OF SPOUSE AND IDENTITY LOSS. . . . DYING
PARENT AND UNFINISHED BUSINESS. . . . "CONSPIRACY
OF SILENCE"—WHAT IT IS AND WHAT TO DO ABOUT
IT. . . . NEED FOR TOUCH AND SHARING THE LAST
HUMAN EXPERIENCE.

There is one important fact we all know about
our lives and yet all tend to deny. That fact is the
passage of time, and old age brings us all closer to
dying and death—the last, inevitable, great experience of life. Do you remember that children's chant
that accompanied the rope-skipping game many of
us played as kids? It went something like this (in
rhythmic cadence):

Mo-ther, Mo-ther, will I die?
Yes, my child, and so will I!

There it is: the fact of death! Even children are aware
of it, in a vague, uncertain way. Like the fact of sex,
the fact of death cannot be hidden or persistently
denied. At worst, it can only be masked and distorted.

It is interesting that earlier cultures and societies never attempted to deny death. They may have developed curious and even strange rituals, but these were all intended to help people face the reality of death and to help them cope in some fashion with the pain of dying and bereavement. We, in our Western culture, have a history of being a dynamic, assertive society that places a premium on youth, beauty, and health. So it's not hard to see why so many taboos about death—even when it comes to talking about it—have grown up among us.

Right at the outset we can perhaps clear the air by acknowledging that dying and death are not a popular subject. Many people find the subject unpleasant and distasteful. They feel uncomfortable even thinking about it, to say nothing of discussing it. Perhaps such persons, having read the heading of this chapter, will decide to skip this section altogether and so will not have gotten this far.

But do they have the right notion? Is this too depressing a note upon which to end this book? I think not! There are at least two good reasons why you should spend some time thinking about this matter. The first is that your elderly are already forced to face the losses of their own kin and peers through death. That kind of loss is an especially severe psychological blow to your aged. Without doubt you keenly wish to be able to help and support them in those dark hours in as effective a way as you can.

The second reason may be even more immediate and personal for you. Inevitably you must yourself face the dying and death of your parents. That is not likely to be a simple, easy event in your life. The basic question for you right now is precisely the one posed at the beginning of this chapter, How will you handle that dying and death when it happens?

The first and most realistic answer to the question is that you must come to terms with your own mortality and your own dying before you can truly handle anyone else's dying and death with any degree of understanding. In other words, if you discover yourself to be uneasy, distressed, or frightened over the prospects of your own demise, inevitable as that will be some day, you are not going to be able to cope very well with another person's end of life. You will find yourself uneasy, distressed, or frightened about the loss, which only serves to remind you of your prospects. This doesn't mean to suggest that everyone should come to feel as cozy when they think of dying as they do when planning to attend a local cinema. It does mean that you need to examine as thoughtfully as you can your feelings about death, and especially the process of dying.

Practically all the surveys that have asked people in all walks of life questions about death and dying report an overwhelming number of people who say they are less apprehensive about death itself than they are about the *process* of dying—that is, most people (when they think about it at all!) worry most about what they believe to be the pain, possible disfigurement (through disease or surgery), personal isolation (as in a hospital away from family), and similar traumas and indignities associated with dying. The notion of death with dignity is a real, deep-seated concern and not just a passing aspect of the popular culture.

What is also important about this self-inventory is that it is not merely a head trip, or what we *think* or *believe* about dying. Coming to terms with your own mortality has to do with a feelings trip, or what we *experience emotionally* about such events. We all need to become not less sensitive but more sensitive about our feelings concerning dying and death. One quite effective way of accomplishing just that is to write down on paper your feelings—your philosophy, if you will—about life and death. Talking at some length to someone you can trust as a patient and sympathetic listener will accomplish much the same thing. In the course of this process, you will want to outline what it is you want out of life, why you have such desires and beliefs, how you think you will react to your own death, and why you think that is so.

That's step one. The second step is to go over whatever previous experiences you have had with death—funerals, wakes, hospitals, sitting at a bedside, things you've read or heard, films you have seen—perhaps even some close brushes with death yourself. What impressions did you get from these experiences, and most important, how did they make you feel? Why did they make you feel that way? All of this is likely to be most useful and meaningful to you if you have the opportunity, in addition, to go over your feelings with another person or persons willing to do the same thing. The idea, of course, is to explore, uncover, and discuss your own emotions and attitudes about dying and death rather than keep them hidden away.

Given substantial progress in dealing with your own reluctance and fears about facing dying and death, how can you help your aging parents come to grips with this highly sensitive, emotional issue? Commonly, there are two areas where they are most likely to require the greatest amount of support. One is when they face the loss of a dear relative or close friend. The other is when they themselves are living through their own last weeks, hours, moments. Let's consider each in turn.

It goes almost without saying that the loss of a dearly loved spouse is the most severe blow to the heart that any human being experiences. Whether the relationship has endured for many years or is of shorter duration, the attachment is deep and the pain of loss profound. A close second to that kind of loss is the death of a child or the death of a dear friend. Such losses produce the need to cope with bereavement. Grieving is the natural, normal response to bereavement. When a love tie is severed, an emotional and behavioral reaction is set in motion. We call that reaction grief, although we do not always recognize grief responses for what they truly are.

You might find your aged parent handling grief by indulging in an unusual amount of complaints of a physical nature. You might begin hearing a lot about aches and pains—sometimes very specific, sometimes expressing a rather vague kind of physical discomfort. All of these, of course, would appear to be good reasons to go see a physician. If the doctor cannot immediately put his finger on a physical cause of the complaint, you needn't be surprised. The pain and distress is very real to your grieving oldster, but it is the distress of bereavement that you are observing, the pain of a wounded heart. Such physical expressions of grief are very much like those that attend physical illness. Even the way we talk about grief demonstrates that. We speak of the loss of a loved one as a "blow" (as indeed it is to the spirit), and later on we talk about the "wound healing."

The loss of a spouse may have any one of a number of meanings. The loss of a spouse can mean the loss of a companion, a confidant, a sexual partner, an audience, a gardener, a cook, a bed warmer, an accountant, a source of income, a social secretary, a social buffer, and so on. Loss of a spouse (or a very close friend) can leave your elderly parent feeling as if a piece of his life were literally torn away. It is no fantasy to feel as if a part of oneself is gone, as if one's identity is somehow blurred.

That's why it is not uncommon for a grieving oldster to show anger after the death. The one who has died may be the object of anger (as if to say, "What right did he [or she] have to do this to me, to desert me like this?"). Anyone—even you—may become the target of anger, annoyance, or irritation. When that does happen, your simple acknowledgment that you recognize and understand the pain and sense of loss can be very helpful and healing. Even more so can be your quiet invitation to talk about feelings, about grief, and about loss. Sometimes family members are extremely reluctant to extend such an invitation because they are trying to protect the person from grief. They don't want to stir up the pain or keep the wounds open. They would like matters to smooth over and quiet down as quickly as possible. In other words, many people are not very comfortable in the presence of grief.

Probably that is why there is a natural inclination for people to avoid those who are bereaved, sad, and depressed. Many are uneasy about being around widows and widowers, especially in the months following their loss, because it is hard to know what to do and what to say that won't sound awkward, clumsy, or trite. Nonetheless, it *is* comforting and reassuring for persons who grieve to hear an expression of sincere concern about and acknowledgment of their sadness. One of the most powerful ingredients in the salve that heals a sorrowing heart is the simple, sincerely extended invitation to share the feelings of loss, to talk about that person who is gone.

Grieving, especially if it is openly expressed and shared grieving, is the process by which intense emotional ties to a dead person are gradually loosened and finally cut. The funeral, the rituals, visits by friends—all provoke memories of the one who has died. It is enormously supporting and healing if you can invite and listen to reminiscing about what has gone before. Grief is the normal reaction to bereavement. Loneliness is the reaction to deprivation. Just exactly how your elder reacts to such deprivation will depend in large measure upon how your parent views himself and how adequately he (or she) has been able to cope with being deprived in the past.

Talking about the one your aged parent has lost is only the first phase. The process of grieving can go on for months. It may involve a widow's going through the dead husband's clothing or other personal effects, or a widower's putting together a memorial scrapbook or album, planting a tree, or retracing a well-remembered journey. All this will stimulate an intense image of the deceased spouse and feeling about the death. All this, too, may be a very necessary part of the grief-work for your elder.

Being deprived of one thing or another is, of course, a part of living and a most common human experience. Some come to terms with the particular experience very well. Others are not so successful; that is, they may appear to come to terms with such feelings, but hidden away inside, behind a brave smile, may be stockpiled a great deal of resentment, hurt, and anger. When that's the case, you shouldn't be too surprised on the occasion of deprivation caused by death to see such persons indulge themselves rather luxuriously in a warm bath of self-pity. And let's face it. It is very difficult to deal with self-pity—whether it's our own or someone else's.

It's difficult to deal with someone else's because self-pity is very likely to arouse your own feelings of resentment, even against your parent. This is true especially if it appears that your parent has a great deal going for him, for example, much love and support and a lot of compensations. That's just the kind of situation that is likely to make you very impatient, annoyed, irritated, and even angry. And who can be comfortable with feelings like that toward a grieving parent? So on top of everything else you end up also feeling guilty. Perhaps more productive than trying to deal with self-pity head on would be to deal with what underlies self-pity, namely the feelings of hurt and resentment. Where such feelings exist and you are successful in making it "safe" for your oldster to *share* such feelings, experience demonstrates that you are about two-thirds of the way toward resolution.

I mentioned earlier that grief may be expressed indirectly sometimes through physical complaints. We should now add to that the fact that grief and self-pity can surface in the form of actual (not imagined) physical ills. No one is certain whether bereavement always directly causes illness or whether it may aggravate a predisposition or condition already present (like heart trouble). But you can be certain that it's common for emotional stress to give rise to physical illness. And a broken heart is an emotional crisis. The stress of bereavement, therefore, can have a direct connection to the sudden occurrence of headaches, digestive upsets, undue fatigue, bouts of insomnia, rheumatism, and a host of other ailments. Even heart attacks and cancer are potentially triggered or aggravated by such major losses. What in effect you are doing by reaching out warmly and sympathetically to your grieving kin is helping to contain or reduce the intolerable stress levels of bereavement, and therefore lessening possible physical ills.

Don't be unduly frightened if you observe your grieving parent "searching" for a spouse lost by death. One widow wrote, "Everywhere I go, I keep searching for him . . . in crowds, in church, in the supermarkets. I keep scanning the faces." Or you may observe illusions that sometimes accompany bereavement: hearing his (or her) voice or calling out the name of the dead spouse as if the spouse were present. These things are not craziness. They are signs of grief. You may also observe much crying. The weeping may not necessarily be crying for the spouse. Such crying may be your parent's way of giving voice to feelings of helplessness, the need for closeness, and the need for reassurance.

If we now agree that the grief process ordinarily works to loosen the emotional ties with the one who has died, it should be quite understandable what the next phase of adapting to loss is all about. A bit earlier

I indicated that losing a well-loved spouse or friend may be very much like having a piece of oneself torn away. That's not mere rhetoric. Almost every widow or widower can testify to some experience of being treated differently than before, somehow, following the death of a spouse. People who have experienced this say that it's like being out of place, like being a different person, almost like being tainted by the death of a spouse.

In certain earlier cultures the stigma of surviving a dead spouse was very real and reactions were very openly displayed. A. L. Cochran—in a fascinating article, "A Little Widow Is a Dangerous Thing," published in the *International Journal of Psychoanalysis* vol. 17 (1936)—offered this remarkable description:

> Among the Shuswap [tribe] of British Columbia, widows and widowers are forbidden to touch their own bodies; the cups and cooking utensils which they use may be used by no one else. They build a sweathouse by a creek, sweat there all night, and bathe regularly, after which they must rub their bodies with branches of spruce. No hunter comes near such mourners for their presence is considered unlucky.

We don't, of course, throw survivors on the funeral pyre of their departed. But we often still find it difficult to fully accept them and their need to mourn. We sometimes still treat grieving as if it were a weakness, a self-indulgence, a kind of bad habit, instead of an emotional and psychological necessity. And we still often treat the survivor as a displaced person, as if, bearing the taint of death, he is unlucky. We don't burn our widows. We pity and avoid them as much as decently possible.

It is clear, then, why the bereaved elder, in going through the grieving process, also needs all the help and support available to establish a new identity. Part of our identity as unique human beings is established and confirmed through our family and friends. When that network is disrupted by death, it must be repaired or reestablished.

You can't give back a dead spouse or friend, obviously. But you can encourage and help your parent to substitute and to find replacements. Community resources are available (religious groups, fraternal organizations, recreational and special interest groups, for example). This is where one not only does things but meets people. Taking hold of new activities and cultivating new interests (as offered by a rich variety of community educational programs for instance) are among the ways a bereaved oldster can go about establishing a new identity.

This leads us to an even touchier subject. How do you deal with your aging parent when he or she is dying? It would be sheer nonsense to talk as if there were "rules" to cover so individual and personal an experience as this. No one else can point out to you more clearly than you know on your own how much hinges upon the kind and quality of the relationship you now have and have had with your parent. The emotions you encounter at the end of life of your parent cannot but be influenced by how close or how distant you have been to each other.

Another strong influence will be what each wants from the other. These wants on the part of the parent and son or daughter are not necessarily identical. Sometimes an elderly parent wants something (like a great deal of attention) from a middle-aged child that the child neither wants nor is prepared to give. That works reversely too. That kind of situation more often than not is the net result of a long family history. There may be deep-rooted resentments or a strong sense of having suffered certain indignities or unfairness because of the other, feelings that have festered and throbbed in the mind and have never been fully resolved. Such feelings were never resolved because they were never discussed openly and frankly.

But the feelings are there, and both parties sense it. Aged parent or middle-aged child or both may not understand why this is so because they don't understand or fully appreciate what's in the mind of the other. What all of this suggests is that you may well have to face, at the end of your parent's life, some important personal unfinished business. This is precisely the soil that breeds feelings of guilt, that is, a sense of being an unworthy, "bad" child or an unworthy, "bad" parent.

It is probably much easier and simpler for an outsider to tell you what not to do than what you should do. Let me begin, then, with that. Almost everyone who has been closely associated with dying persons in a personal way agrees that there is everything to be gained and nothing to be lost by avoiding the "conspiracy of silence." What is the conspiracy of silence? It is acting as if the dying elderly parent is not really dying. That happens when a physician, nurse, relative, friend, or anyone refuses to acknowledge what the reality is. The physician, for example, may gloss over or mask the facts (for whatever reason) about what clearly appears to be a terminal illness.

Obviously there are very fine lines separating the communication of plain facts, prospects, appropriate reassurance, and false or unreasonable hopes. It is not rare for an individual (although less common among aging persons) to deny the facts when he is informed of his terminal illness. But in the long run it's no service to that individual to play the same game. At the same time we should recognize that most persons who are dying know it, even if shocked and frightened by that knowledge. Shouldn't those persons have the opportunity to prepare for the end and have lots of moral support in doing so?

If your dying mother, for example, wants to talk to you sometime about "What will happen when . . ." and you cut her off with a "Don't talk like that, Mother. You're going to be with us for a long time" (or "be home from the hospital in spring"), no matter how good your intentions, you have entered into a conspiracy of silence. You have, in effect, made yourself unavailable for listening. You are, indirectly, saying, "I don't want to talk about it." By so doing, you have forced your dying parent into the position of facing this last, great experience of living in emotional isolation, abandoned to facing concerns, fears, and apprehensions all alone. Because there are those who *do* talk and listen to dying persons and tell us what it's like, we now understand how terribly cruel and inhuman the conspiracy of silence can be when it is used with those who are dying. Without doubt dying persons have many concerns and fears. With whom can they share? To whom can they talk about the possibility of pain, about funeral arrangements, about memorials, about what will happen to a lifetime of treasured goods (books, furniture, handicrafts, recipes—whatever), about a beloved pet, about the future of the grandchildren? The list of concerns, obviously, is endless.

The irony of the conspiracy of silence as it is too often practiced is that it is quite easy to avoid. All you need do is offer a gentle, sincere invitation: "Dear, would you like to talk about it? If you do, I would like to listen." Some will accept this kind invitation at once and begin to share what's on the mind and in the heart. Others, on the other hand, may refuse—at first. Those who do may accept the invitation later on, when they are more prepared to do so. Often your just being there, holding the hand of a dying parent in a warm, tender clasp, can make an enormous difference. The point is by such a response you are not blocking or isolating your parent. You are saying by word and action that your dying parent need not face this trying experience alone.

The second important reason for avoiding the conspiracy of silence has to do with the matter of unfinished business mentioned earlier. The conspiracy of silence with respect to a dying parent prevents finishing such personal business, with unhappy emotional consequences that can linger for years. Not long ago, after concluding a lecture on death and dying, I was approached by a middle-aged man who obviously felt stirred by some of the issues discussed. He described his father, who had died a year previously, as a man who had been a "good" but a rather stern father, one who had never been very demonstrative or directly affectionate with his children as they grew up. This man spoke quietly of his deep yearning for some demonstration, some token, of affection from his father over the years and of his inability to say that clearly and directly to his dad.

With misty eyes he related some facts about the final weeks and hours of his father's life, how desperately he wanted to tell his father that he cared. He also described the emotion-laden silences between them when he sat with his dying parent and how strongly he felt that his dad wanted to say "something" to him (he just "knew" that his father wanted to tell his son that he cared too). How poignant it was in that moment when this man described his father's dying at last that neither could bring himself to share the most important thing of all. And even then, a year after that death, this man continued to be haunted by a silence between them that so easily could have been, and yet never was, broken.

Sometimes the death of a parent occurs suddenly, at an unexpected moment, even though the parent is quite old. But more often the signals and signs of dying are all there for some time. Often it is a process drawn out, sometimes for weeks or even months. And that time can be, if you are prepared and willing to make it so, a time for completing unfinished business—a time rich in listening, in sharing, in intimacy. Yes it can even be a time rich in planning and growth for you both. Those who have experienced being with a dying parent right to the end (preferably at home rather than agonizing in a strange hospital waiting room for an announcement of death) all describe how deeply satisfying it is to end the relationship with a parent in this close and initimate manner.

8

You Are Not On Your Own

One important underlying message of this handbook is that your concerns and worries as well as your hopes and dreams regarding your aging parents are shared by a great many other middle-aged sons and daughters. Particular details and circumstances may vary somewhat from family to family. But it is reassuring to know and understand that you are not alone in your concerns and not really unique in your situation. Without exception, the several themes as well as related issues discussed here are actually quite common and are repeated over and over again in one form or another throughout our society.

Not only are you not alone *in* this, neither are you entirely *on* your own in this. There still exist far too many myths and stereotypes about the aging process and about aged people. Unfortunately, far too many professional people still remain less than enthusiastic (or even knowledgeable) about serving the special needs of elderly people in appropriate ways. Not only that, it is plain for all to see that our public policy has a long way to go before it catches up with the most useful, relevant information at hand about how to help middle-aged sons and daughters assist their aging parents. Still, in spite of all this, the scene is changing and in many ways for the better. There are at least some professionals you can turn to, if and when needed, who are experienced in working with the aged and understanding of their special needs and who are not patronizing toward the old.

You will find such professionals in medicine, in law, in psychology, and among the clergy of all faiths. You will find such persons in dentistry and in public administration and among legislators, licensed and practical nurses, physical and occupational therapists, medical and psychiatric social workers, home and community aides, recreation specialists, educators at all levels, speech pathologists, dietitians and nutritionists, sex therapists, pre- and post-retirement counselors, information and referral specialists, long-term care and nursing-home professionals, and job placement (vocational) counselors. And the number of such trained professionals is growing. You will immediately recognize that this is not a complete listing. This will, however, indicate to you the rather wide variety of special skills that may be available to fill some particular need or assist you with some special concern. Professionals with specialized skills who are also experienced and interested in working with the aged might not always be available in every community. This poses a problem. You may well wonder how to go about identifying and locating such persons.

There are at least three avenues for you to follow in order to discover what help is available when you need it. One is at the local (neighborhood or city) level. Another will lead you to the state level. And the third brings you to resources available at the national level.

At the local level you can contact an individual who is identified as a member of the professional field in which you seek help. Simply ask if you can be put in touch with a professional who can provide whatever assistance you and your aging parent may require. You needn't feel timid about making such inquiries, nor should you be reluctant to ask the questions that will get you the information you want. After all, you need information to make judgments, and you need sufficient information to make informed decisions. There are persons whose job it is to help you.

It is not presumptuous, either, to try to find out something about the attitudes of the professionals whose assistance you seek. Don't hesitate, for instance, to ask if a physician is familiar with and experienced in working with aged persons. That can be of crucial importance. Physical and health factors (particularly the use of a number of commonly prescribed drugs) are often significantly different for the eighty-year-old than they are for the twenty-seven-year-old. If you pursue such a dialogue with a physician, you are most likely to pick up some clues about the physician's interest in working with an elderly person. If you hear statements to the effect, "Oh, that's just old age . . . there's nothing anyone can do," you can be fairly sure that's one professional who is inclined to write off your parent because of age. And that ought to alert you at least to the possibility that that professional, apart from other considerations of competence, is not the appropriate provider of service for you and your aging parent.

The very same considerations, of course, apply equally to any other professional you may seek out for help, whether it be a psychologist, nurse, social worker, home aide or helper, dentist, nursing-home administrator, or whoever. You are surely entitled to discover, right at the outset, something about the professional person's attitudes and experience in dealing with the aged because under most circumstances it can make a big difference. A professional degree and experience with a younger population in and of itself may not be sufficient basis for serving the needs of the aged.

There are other sources to turn to for help. You can get in touch with local groups, centers, and agencies that identify themselves as providing direct services for the aged or information about such services. Usually, such centers and agencies are funded by public taxes, but some are supported by private and religious organizations. You will find them in all large urban areas and in many smaller communities and rural areas as well.

Most communities now have an Area Agency on Aging (they're sometimes called Triple A's). These were set up about two years ago not to provide direct services so much as to coordinate the many different services to the elderly in a given community. The Triple A's (don't confuse them with the auto club) should be an excellent source of information about available services and how to locate appropriate professionals.

Every state in the nation has a department of aging. The names may vary slightly: some are called simply Department of Aging, Commission on Aging, Office of Aging, or the like. Whatever it's called, you should have little trouble identifying it. Your local city hall ought to be able to give you the name of the person in charge, the address, and the phone number. A large number of cities also have a special city office or department designated as a resource on aging.

Sometimes these are called the Mayor's Committee (or Commission) on Aging. Every city has a department of health and most have a department of social services. Within these departments you should find some section that concerns itself specially with the elderly. These can provide information for you too.

Bear in mind that many communities, particularly large urban areas in all parts of the country, experience almost an embarrassment of riches when it comes to services and programs serving the aged. In cities of a million population or more, there are literally hundreds of such services and programs— some separate and distinct, some overlapping—that are run by federal, state, and city agencies; by volunteer groups (large and small); and by religious and fraternal organizations. In addition there are many self-help groups. It would be an enormous task (and probably not helpful) to try to offer a list here.

As a small sample, however, you can look in your telephone book or call your local branch or main library for the numbers or locations of

1. **Day activities centers.** These centers usually offer certain activities (such as handicrafts, cooking classes), but not the same package of services as the multiservice center. Many are sponsored by religious groups on a part-time basis.

2. **Multiservice centers for the elderly.** These are beginning to sprout up in many communities. They are usually open from about 7:30 or 8:00 A.M. daily (except weekends) until late afternoon. They are a little different from day activities centers in that they provide a number of services, such as health and dental screening, legal and personal counseling,

group discussions, educational classes, hot lunches, exercise programs, handicraft activities, or some combination of these. Check the local centers about hours and specific services offered.

3. **Meals-on-Wheels.** This is a federally funded nutrition program that delivers a hot meal, usually once a day, to elderly persons who cannot easily leave their homes.

4. **Senior citizens centers.** These are usually sponsored by municipal departments of recreation and parks. They simply provide attractive and convenient space where elderly persons can gather during the day to play games together (cards, bingo, shuffleboard). At times special discussions or programs are arranged.

5. **Dial-a-ride.** In some communities this service provides door-to-door transportation for the aged on request.

6. **Nutrition centers.** These were established by federal funding to furnish a hot noon meal to elderly persons who come to the center (often a school or church auditorium). A very important opportunity is provided to meet people, make new friends, and socialize over lunch.

7. **RSVP.** This stands for Retired Senior Volunteer Program. It is designed to enlist the aid of retired persons in contacting the "hidden" elderly, that is, those older persons who don't get into the community but stay in their own homes.

8. **DOVES.** This stands for Dedicated Older Volunteers in Educational Services. As the name indicates, this older volunteer corps tries to encourage and provide a variety of adult educational opportunities.

9. **Foster Grandparents Program.** This is another action program. Persons over sixty years of age provide guidance and companionship to mentally, physically, or emotionally handicapped children.
10. **Home health agencies.** These service agencies go by a variety of names in different locales. They provide services for incapacitated elderly in their own homes and also information about where to locate home helpers, visiting nurses, part-time housekeeping help, and so on.

This is just the tip of the iceberg with respect to many different and related resources upon which to draw. The local department of health, for example, can furnish you with locations of licensed nursing homes and perhaps retirement residences. The department is not likely to give you an evaluation or rating, only location.

Nor should you overlook, as a resource, the religious groups that in most communities can provide information and possibly some direct service. Catholic social service agencies, interfaith coalitions, the Jewish Federation, the Jewish Family Service, as well as community mental health centers, all have as part of their overall programs some commitment to serving the aged. They are easily reached by telephone and can assist, inform, and refer you for the help you and your aging parent seek. Also individual Catholic parishes, Protestant churches, and Jewish synagogues can be good sources. You have to try them. Some of them provide supportive services as well as useful information.

A growing number of city and community colleges in many areas now have some staff who are specialists in aging. City school systems now almost universally have a wide variety of adult education programs specifically geared to and located for the convenience of elderly people. City and community colleges are beginning to offer in similar fashion courses specifically designed for the elderly. It may well be worth your while to contact these educational institutions.

A number of universities have now developed centers on aging (in some instances called gerontology centers). Although the colleges and universities with such gerontology centers devote their major efforts to research and the training of professionals in the field, they have many experts in aging on their staffs and are an excellent resource. Some of them do provide expert, professional counseling services to the aged and their families.

The following is a partial list of institutions in the United States that have programs on aging that can be valuable resources. In order not to overlook a possibility, you should check with colleges and universities near you.

- **University of Arizona,** Tucson, Arizona
- **Ethel Percy Andrus Gerontology Center, University of Southern California,** Los Angeles, California. The largest multidisciplinary center in the nation devoted exclusively to the study of aging. It also offers individual and group counseling for the elderly and their families on a regular basis.
- **University of California,** San Diego, California
- **Florida State University,** Tallahassee, Florida
- **Georgia State University,** Atlanta, Georgia
- **University of Hawaii,** Honolulu, Hawaii

- **Committee on Human Development, The University of Chicago,** Chicago, Illinois
- **Aging Center, University of Maryland,** College Park, Maryland
- **The University of Michigan,** Ann Arbor, Michigan
- **Wayne State University,** Detroit, Michigan
- **Oakland University,** Rochester, Michigan
- **University of Minnesota,** Minneapolis, Minnesota
- **University of Missouri,** Columbia, Missouri
- **Washington University,** St. Louis, Missouri
- **Center on Aging, Syracuse University,** Syracuse, New York
- **Center for the Study of Aging and Human Development, Duke University,** Durham, North Carolina
- **Miami University,** Oxford, Ohio
- **Gerontology Center, University of Oregon,** Salem, Oregon
- **Temple University,** Philadelphia, Pennsylvania
- **The Pennsylvania State University,** University Park, Pennsylvania
- **Center for Studies in Aging, North Texas State University,** Denton, Texas
- **University of Utah,** Salt Lake City, Utah
- **University of Washington,** Seattle, Washington
- **West Virginia University,** Morgantown, West Virginia
- **University of Wisconsin,** Madison, Wisconsin
- **The Catholic University of America,** Washington, D.C.

Finally, there are a number of national societies and organizations that will gladly provide you with information and that can also direct you to local resources. These are

1. **Administration on Aging (AOA)**
   Office on Human Development
   U. S. Dept. of Health, Education and Welfare
   400 Sixth Street, S.W.
   Washington, D.C. 20201
   This is a government agency responsible for the administration of the Older Americans Act. It publishes a periodical called *Aging*.

2. **American Geriatrics Society, Inc.**
   10 Columbus Circle, Room 1470
   New York, New York 10019
   This society encourages and promotes research in the fields of aging and clinical geriatrics. It also publishes a monthly journal to disseminate information regarding diagnosis, treatment, and prevention of acute and chronic disease in the elderly.

3. **American Medical Association**
   Committee on Aging
   535 North Dearborn Street
   Chicago, Illinois 60610
   The committee states that it works to promote positive health care and meaningful living for all older persons; to encourage the development and maintenance of programs for older persons that emphasize the importance of self-help and independence; and to provide guidance for policies governing the medical, nursing, and related health services provided in nursing homes and other long-term care facilities.

4. **The American Society for**
   Geriatric Dentistry
   431 Oakdale Avenue, 9B
   Chicago, Illinois 60657

One of the main purposes of this society is the promotion of postgraduate education of the dental practitioner in gerontology and geriatrics, medical and dental.

5. **The Gerontological Society**
   One Dupont Circle, N.W., Suite 520
   Washington, D.C. 20036
   This is a national organization of researchers, educators, and professionals in the field of aging. It promotes the scientific study of aging; fosters application of research to practice; uses research in the development of public policy; and develops the qualifications of gerontologists by setting high standards of professional ethics, conduct, education, and achievement. It publishes two journals.

6. **National Association of Area Agencies on Aging**
   Central Bank Building
   Suite 350
   Huntsville, Alabama 35801
   and
   National Association of State Units on Aging
   State Office Building
   1123 Eutaw Street
   Baltimore, Maryland 21201
   See earlier remarks about Triple A's.

7. **National Senior Citizens Law Center**
   1709 West Eighth Street
   Los Angeles, California 90017

8. **Legal Research and Services for the Elderly**
   1511 K Street, N.W.
   Washington, D.C. 20005

9. **National Caucus on the Black Aged**
   1725 DeSales Street, N.W.
   Washington, D.C. 20036

10. **National Council for Homemaker–Home Health Aide Services, Inc.**

67 Irving Place, 6th Floor
New York, New York 10003

11. **National Interfaith Coalition on Aging**
    222 South Downey Avenue
    Indianapolis, Indiana 46219

12. **National Council of Senior Citizens (NCSC)**
    1511 K Street, N.W.
    Washington, D.C. 20005
    This organization is an affiliation of some
    3,500 local senior citizens clubs with a
    combined membership of over three million
    people, actively working for a better life for
    the aged. It makes available specific
    information (through its monthly publication,
    Senior Citizens News) on services and
    programs at local, state, and national levels.

13. **National Council on the Aging (NCOA)**
    1828 L Street, N.W., Suite 504
    Washington, D.C. 20036
    This is a nonprofit organization that serves as
    a central resource providing information,
    materials, and technical assistance to
    professionals in the field of aging. The council
    works with other organizations to develop
    concern for older people and methods and
    resources to meet their needs. Its programs
    include the National Institute of Senior
    Centers, national voluntary organizations for
    independent living by the aged, and the
    National Media Resource Center on Aging. It
    publishes two periodicals.

14. **American Association of Retired Persons/
    National Retired Teachers Association
    (AARP/NRTA)**
    These are nonprofit educational, philanthropic,
    and scientific membership organizations
    serving all older persons. They have active

membership chapters in every state and a total membership approaching nine million. They award grants to universities for action research aimed at producing information of a practical nature. They actively lobby for legislation of benefit to the elderly. They offer low-cost vitamins and drugs through pharmacy services to their members. Both organizations support educational (preretirement) programs. They publish two excellent illustrated magazines—*Modern Maturity* and *Dynamic Maturity*. Membership fees are modest.

15. **American Association of Homes for the Aging (AAHA)**
    374 National Press Building
    14th & F Streets, N W.
    Washington, D.C: 20045
    and
    American College of Nursing Home Administrators (ACNHA)
    4650 East-West Highway
    Washington, D.C. 20014
    and
    Associated University Programs in Health Administration (AUPHA)
    Office of Long-Term Care, Suite 312
    1755 Massachusetts Avenue, N.W.
    Washington, D.C. 20036
    These organizations will provide various information including some on nursing homes and long-term care. AAHA and ACNHA have state chapters made up of practicing long-term care professionals, who can provide useful information.

And, of course, any one of the hundreds of Social Security branches is available to give information about Social Security, Supplemental Security Income, Medicare, and Medicaid entitlements.

SUGGESTIONS FOR FURTHER READING
(informative, nontechnical, and inspirational)

Butler, Robert. *Why Survive! Being Old in America.* New York: Harper & Row, 1975.

Comfort, Alex. *A Good Age.* New York: Crown Publishers, Inc., 1976.

de Beauvoir, Simone. *The Coming of Age.* New York: G. B. Putnam's Sons, 1972; New York: Penguin, 1973.

Puner, Morton. *To the Good Long Life: What We Know About Growing Old.* New York: Universe Books, 1974.

Sarton, May. *As We Are Now.* New York: W. W. Norton & Co., Inc., 1973.

Scott-Maxwell, Florida. *The Measure of My Days.* New York: Alfred A. Knopf, Inc., 1968.